AN OUTLINE OF THE PHONOLOGY AND MORPHOLOGY OF OLD PROVENÇAL

AN OUTLINE OF THE PHONOLOGY AND MORPHOLOGY OF OLD PROVENÇAL

C. H. GRANDGENT
Former Professor of Romance Languages at Harvard University

Richmond
TIGER XENOPHON
MMIX

This edition first published
in 2009 by
Tiger Xenophon
50 Albert Road
Richmond
Surrey TW10 6DP
United Kingdom

Tiger Xenophon is an imprint of
Tiger of the Stripe

ISBN 978-1-904799-27-6

Printed in the US and UK by
Lightning Source

PREFACE.

THIS book, which is intended as a guide to students of Romance Philology, represents the result of desultory labors extending through a period of twenty years. My first introduction to the scientific pursuit of Provençal linguistics was a course given by Paul Meyer at the École des Chartes in the winter of 1884–85. Since then I have been collecting material both from my own examination of texts and from the works of those philologists who have dealt with the subject. Besides the large Grammars of the Romance Languages by Diez and by Meyer-Lübke, I have utilized H. Suchier's *Die französische und provenzalische Sprache* (in Gröber's *Grundriss der romanischen Philologie*, I, 561), the *Introduzione grammaticale* in V. Crescini's *Manualetto provenzale*, the *Abriss der Formenlehre* in C. Appel's *Provenzalische Chrestomathie*, and many special treatises to which reference will be made in the appropriate places. Conscious of many imperfections in my work, I shall be grateful for corrections.

I have confined myself to the old literary language, believing that to be of the greatest importance to a student of Romance Philology or of Comparative Literature, and fearing lest an enumeration of modern forms, in addition to the ancient, might prove too bewildering. I should add that neither my own knowledge nor the material at my disposal is adequate to a satisfactory presentation of the living idioms of southern France. These dialects have, however, been investigated for the light they throw on the geographical distribution of phonetic variations; my chief source of information has been F. Mistral's monumental *Dictionnaire provençal-français*. Catalan and Franco-Provençal have been considered only incidentally. I have not dealt with word-formation, because one of my students is preparing a treatise on that subject.

Readers desiring a brief description of Provençal literature are referred to H. Suchier and A. Birch-Hirschfeld, *Geschichte der französischen Literatur*, pp. 56–96; A. Stimming, in Gröber's *Grundriss der romanischen Philologie*, II, ii, pp. 1–69; and A. Restori, *Letteratura provenzale*. For a more extended account of the poets they should consult *Die Poesie der Troubadours* and the *Leben und Werke der Troubadours* by F. Diez; and *The Troubadours at Home* by J. H. Smith. The poetic ideals are discussed by G. Paris in *Romania*, XII, pp. 516–34; and with great fulness by L. F. Mott in *The System of Courtly Love*. The beginnings of the literature are treated by A. Jeanroy in his *Origines de la poésie lyrique en France au moyen âge*, reviewed by G. Paris in a series of important articles in the *Journal des Savants* (November and December, 1891, and March and July, 1892) reprinted separately in 1892 under the same title as Jeanroy's book. Contributions by A. Restori to several volumes of the *Rivista musicale italiana* deal with Provençal music; some tunes in modern notation are to be found in J. H. Smith's *Troubadours at Home*, and in the *Archiv für das Studium der neueren Sprachen*, CX (New Series X), 110 (E. Bohn). Aside from the editions of individual poets, the best collections of verses are those of C. Appel, *Provenzalische Chrestomathie*; V. Crescini, *Manualetto provenzale*; and K. Bartsch, *Chresto-*

mathie provençale. Earlier and larger anthologies are M. Raynouard's *Choix des poésies originales des troubadours*, and C. A. F. Mahn's *Werke der Troubadours* and *Gedichte der Troubadours.* The only dictionary of importance for the old language is the *Lexique roman* (six volumes) of M. Raynouard, augmented by the *Supplement-Wörterbuch* of E. Levy (now appearing in instalments). The poetic language of the present day can be studied to advantage in E. Koschwitz's *Grammaire historique de la langue des Félibres.*

C. H. GRANDGENT.

CAMBRIDGE, MASS., NOVEMBER, 1904.

ABBREVIATIONS AND TECHNICAL TERMS.

Abl.: ablative.
Acc.: accusative.
Cl.L.: Classic Latin.
Cond.: conditional.
Cons.: consonant.
Einf.: W. Meyer-Lübke, *Einführung in das Studium der romanischen Sprachwissenschaft*, 1901.
F.: feminine.
Fr.: French.
Free (of vowels): not in position.
Fut.: future.
Gram.: W. Meyer-Lübke, *Grammaire des langues romanes*, 3 vols., 1890–1900.
Grundriss: G. Gröber, *Grundriss der romanischen Philologie*, 2 vols., 1888–1902.
Imp.: imperfect.
Imper.: imperative.
Intertonic (of vowels): following the secondary and preceding the primary accent.
Intervocalic (of consonants): standing between two vowels.
It.: Italian.
Körting: G. Körting, *Lateinisch-romanisches Wörterbuch*, 2d ed., 1901.
Lat.: Latin.
Levy: E. Levy, *Provenzalisches Supplement-Wörterbuch*, 1894—.
Ltblt.: *Literaturblatt für germanische und romanische Philologie*, monthly, Leipzig.
M.: masculine.
Nom.: nominative.
Obj.: objective (case).
Part.: participle.
Perf.: perfect.
Pers.: person.
Phon.: P. Marchot, *Petite phonétique du français prélittéraire*, 1901.
Pl.: plural.
Pr.: Provençal.
Pres.: present.
Pret.: preterit.
Raynouard: M. Raynouard, *Lexique roman*, 6 vols., 1836–44.
Rom.: *Romania*, quarterly, Paris.
Sg.: singular.
V.L.: Vulgar Latin.
Voc.: H. Schuchardt, *Vocalismus des Vulgärlateins*, 3 vols., 1866–68.
Voiced (of consonants): sonant, pronounced with vibration of the glottis.
Voiceless (of consonants): surd, pronounced without glottal vibration.
Vow.: vowel.
Zs.: *Zeitschrift für romanische Philologie*, 4 to 6 nos. a year, Halle.

SIGNS AND PHONETIC SYMBOLS.

N. B.—Phonetic characters not entered in this list are to be pronounced as in Italian. Whenever it is essential to distinguish spelling from pronunciation, *italic* type is used for the former, Roman for the latter.

̣ (under a vowel): close quality.
̨ (under a vowel): open quality.
‒ (over a vowel): long quantity.
˘ (over a vowel): short quantity.
̯ (under a letter): semivowel, not syllabic.
ʹ (over a letter): stress.

ʹ (after a consonant): palatal pronunciation.
* (before a word): conjectural, not found.
> (between words or letters): derivation, the *source* standing at the *open* end.
+: followed by.

ạ: French *â* in *pâte*.
ą̣: French *a* in *patte*.
β: bilabial *v*, as in Spanish.
c: see k.
c′: palatal *k*, as in English *key*.
ð: English *th* in *this*.
ẹ: French *é* in *thé*.
ę: French *ê* in *fête*.
g: English *g* in *go*.
g′: palatal *g*, as in English *geese*.
h: English *h* in *hat*.
ị: French *i* in *si*.
į: English *i* in *pit*.
k: English *k* in *maker*.
k′: see c′.
l′: palatal *l*, as in Italian *figlio*.
n′: palatal *n*, as in Italian *ogni*.
ŋ: English *ng* in *sing*.
ọ: German *ō*, as in *sohn*.
ǫ: German *ŏ*, as in *sonne*.
r′: palatal *r*.
š: English *sh* in *ship*.
þ: English *th* in *thin*.
ụ: German *ū*, as in *gut*.
ų: German *ŭ*, as in *butter*.
ü: French *u* in *pur*.
w: English *w* in *woo*.
χ: German *ch* in *ach*.
y: English *y* in *ye*.
z: English *z* in *crazy*.
ž: French *j* in *jour*.

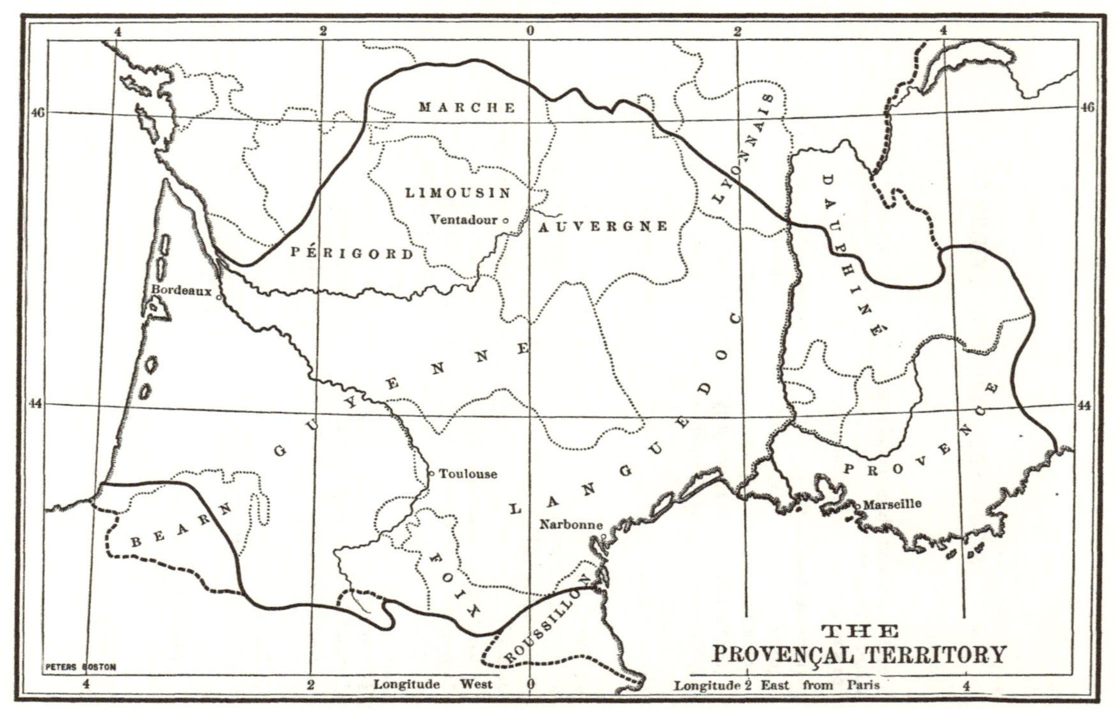
THE
PROVENÇAL TERRITORY
MARCHE
LIMOUSIN
Ventadour
AUVERGNE
LYONNAIS
DAUPHINÉ
PÉRIGORD
Bordeaux
GUYENNE
LANGUEDOC
PROVENCE
Marseille
Toulouse
Narbonne
BEARN
FOIX
ROUSSILLON
Longitude West
Longitude 2 East from Paris
PETERS BOSTON

TABLE OF CONTENTS.

AN OUTLINE OF THE PHONOLOGY AND MORPHOLOGY OF OLD PROVENÇAL.

I. INTRODUCTION.

1. The language here studied is, in the main, that used by the poets of Southern France during the 12th and 13th centuries. The few works that we have earlier than the 12th century must, of course, be utilized for such information as they afford concerning the process of linguistic change; and lacking words or forms must occasionally be sought in writings later than the 13th. Prose literature, moreover, should not be neglected, as it greatly enlarges our vocabulary and throws much light on local divergences. The modern dialects need be cited only to determine the geographical distribution of variations.

2. The extent of the Provençal territory is sufficiently indicated by the map on p. viii. The upper black line separates Provençal on the northwest and north from French, on the northeast from Franco-Provençal; on the east are the Gallo-Italic dialects. The lower black line divides Provençal on the southwest from Basque, on the south from Spanish, on the southeast from Catalan. The boundary line between French and Provençal must be determined somewhat arbitrarily, as there is no distinct natural division; the several linguistic characteristics of each idiom do not end at the

same point, and thus one language gradually shades into the other. The line shown on the map is based on the development of free accented Latin **a**, which remains **a** in Provençal, but is changed to **e** in French. The limits of other phonetic phenomena may be found in Suchier's maps at the back of Vol. I of Gröber's *Grundriss*. There may be seen also a large map showing the place of Provençal among the Romance languages. Consult, furthermore, P. Meyer in *Romania*, XXIV, 529.

3. The Spanish and Gallo-Italic frontiers are more clearly defined, and Basque is entirely distinct. Franco-Provençal and Catalan, on the other hand, are closely related to Provençal and not always easy to divide from it. Catalan, in fact, is often classed as a Provençal dialect; but it is sufficiently different to be studied separately. Franco-Provençal, rated by some philologists as an independent language, has certain characteristics of Provençal and certain features of French, but more of the latter; in some respects it is at variance with both. The Gascon, or southwest, dialects of Provençal differ in many ways from any of the others and present not a few similarities to Spanish[1]; they will, however, be included in our study.

4. The Provençal domain embraces, then, the following old provinces: Provence, Languedoc, Foix, part of Béarn, Gascony, Guyenne, Limousin, most of Marche, Auvergne, the southwestern half of Lyonnais and the southern half of Dauphiné. The native speech in this region varies considerably from place to place, and the local dialects are, for convenience, roughly grouped under the names of the provinces; it should be remembered, however, that the political

[1] See E. Bourciez, *les Mots espagnols comparés aux mots gascons.*

and the linguistic boundaries rarely coincide. For some of the principal dialect differences, see §§ 8 and 10–13.

5. The old poets frequently called their language *lemosí*; and, in fact, the foundation of their literary idiom is the speech of the province of Limousin and the adjacent territory on the north, west, and southwest.[1] The supremacy of this dialect group is apparently due to the fact that it was generally used for composition earlier than any of the others: popular song, in all probability, had its home in the borderland of Marche[2]; religious literature in the vulgar tongue developed in the monasteries of this region; the artistic lyric was cultivated, we know, at the court of Ventadour, and it must have found favor at others. Furthermore, many of the leading troubadours belonged by birth or residence to the Limousin district.

6. The troubadours' verses, as we have them, seldom represent any one dialect in its purity. The poet himself was doubtless influenced both by literary tradition and by his particular local usage, as well as by considerations of rhyme and metre. Moreover, his work, before reaching us, passed through the hands of various intermediaries, who left upon it traces of their own pronunciation. It should be said, also, that the Limousin was not a single dialect, but a group of more or less divergent types of speech. For these reasons we must not expect to find in Provençal a uniform linguistic standard.

7. Neither was there a generally accepted system of orthography. When the vulgar tongue was first written, the

---

[1] See C. Chabaneau, *la Langue et la littérature du Limousin*, in the *Revue des langues romanes*, XXXV, 379.

[2] See G. Paris, *Origines de la poésie lyrique en France au moyen âge.*

Roman letters were used with approximately the same values that they had in Latin, as it was then pronounced. As the Provençal sounds changed, there was a conflict between the spellings first established and new notations based on contemporary speech. Furthermore, many Provençal vowels and consonants had no equivalents in Latin; for these we find a great variety of representations. The signs are very often ambiguous: for instance, *c* before *e* or *i* (as in *cen*, *cinc*) generally stands in the first texts for ts, in the more recent ones for s, the pronunciation having changed; *z* between vowels in early times usually means dz (*plazer*), but later z (*roza*); *i* between vowels (*maiór*) indicates either y or dž (English *j*), according to the dialect; a *g* may signify "hard" g (*gerra*), dž ("soft" *g*: *ges*), or tš (English *ch*: *mieg*). It is probable that for a couple of centuries diphthongs were oftenest written as simple vowels.

8. Some features of the mediæval pronunciation are still obscure. The close ọ was transformed, either during or soon after the literary epoch, into ụ (the sound of French *ou*); hence, when we meet in a late text such a word as *flor*, we cannot be certain whether it is to be sounded flọr or flụr. We do not know at what time Latin ū in southern France took the sound ü (French *u*): some suppose that it was during or shortly before the literary period; if this be true, the letter *u* (as in *tu*, *mur*) may represent in some texts ụ, in others ü. In diphthongs and triphthongs whose first element is written *u* (*cuer*, *fuolha*, *nueu*, *buou*), this letter came to be pronounced in most of the dialects like French *u* in *huit*, while in others it retained the sound of French *ou* in *oui*; we cannot tell exactly when or where, in ancient times, this development occurred. In the diphthongs ue, uo (*luec*, *fuoc*), opinions disagree as to which vowel originally bore the stress; subsequent changes seem to indicate that in the 12th and 13th centuries the practice varied in the different dialects. Old Provençal must have had in some words a peculiar type of r, which was sufficiently palatal in its articulation to call for an i-glide before it (*esclairar*); we do not know precisely how it was formed; in most regions it probably was assimilated to the more usual r as early as the 12th century. The š and ž (palatal s and z) apparently ranged, in the several dialects, between the sounds of French *ch* and *j* on the one hand, and those of German *ch* (in *ich*) and *j* (in *ja*) on the other; the former types were largely assimilated, doubtless by the 13th century, to s and z (*pois*, *maisó*), the latter were not (*poih*, *maió*).

9. The following table comprises the Old Provençal sounds with their usual spellings, the latter being arranged, as nearly as may be, in the order of their frequency. Diphthongs and triphthongs are included in the vowel list, compound consonants in the consonant table. For an explanation of the phonetic symbols, see p. vii. The variant pronunciations are discussed in § 8.

VOWELS.

SOUND.	SPELLINGS.	EXAMPLES.
ạ	*a*	*pan*
ą	*a*	*car*
ai	*ai, ay*	*paire, cays*
au	*au*	*autre*
ẹ	*e*	*pena*
ę	*e*	*cel*
ẹi	*ei, ey*	*vei, veyre*
ęi	*ei, ey*	*seis, teysser*
ẹu	*eu*	*beure*
ęu	*eu*	*breu*
ị	*i, y*	*amic, ydola*

SOUND.	SPELLINGS.	EXAMPLES.
ię	*ie, e*	*quier, velh*
ięi	*iei, iey, ei*	*ieis, lieys, leit*
ięu	*ieu, eu*	*mieu, deus*
ịu	*iu*	*estiu*
ọ (or ụ)	*o, u*	*corre, sun*
ǫ	*o*	*cors*
ọi	*oi, oy*	*conoisser, oyre*
ǫi	*oi, oy*	*pois, poyssán*
ọu	*ou*	*dous*
ǫu	*ou*	*mou*
ụ: see ọ, ü		
ü (or ụ?)	*u*	*mut*
uę, üę	*ue, o?*	*cuec, olh?*
uęi, üęi	*uei, uey, oi?*	*cueissa, pueyssas, oit?*
uęu, üęu	*ueu, ou?*	*nueu, bou?*
üi	*ui, uy*	*cuit, duy*
uǫ, üǫ	*uo, o*	*gruoc, folha*
uǫi, üǫi	*uoi, oi*	*puoi, noit*
uǫu, üǫu	*uou, ou*	*pluou, ou*

CONSONANTS.

SOUND.	SPELLINGS.	EXAMPLES.
b	*b, bb*	*bel, abbat*
d	*d*	*don*
dz	*z, c*	*plazer, dicén*
dž	*i, g, tg, gg, ti, tgi, ih*	*ioc, gen, paratge, viagge, coratie, lotgiar, puihar*
ð	*d*	*veder*
f	*f, ph*	*fer, phizica*
g	*g, gu*	*gras, guan, guerra*
h (Gascon)	*h, f?*	*ham, fe?*[1]
k	*c, qu, k, g*	*cais, quar, quer, ki, longs*[2]
l	*l, ll*	*leu, belleza*

[1] This h (coming from f) is peculiar to Gascon; the other dialects have no h.

[2] *G, b, d* are sounded k, p, t only at the end of a word or before a final s.

SOUND.	SPELLINGS.	EXAMPLES.
l'	*lh, ill, ilh, ll, l, il, yl, yll, li*	*fuelha, meillor, failha, vellar, viel, voil, fiyl, fayllentia, filia*
m	*m, mm*	*mes, commanda*
n	*n, nn*	*nas, annat*
n'	*nh, gn, inh, ign, ing, innh, ingn, ngn, nn, n, in, ng, ynh, ni, ny, nyh*	*cenher, plagner, poinh, seignor, soing, poinnher, fraingner, ongnimen, vinna, franén, soin, sengor, poynh, lenia, senyoria, senyhor*
ŋ	*n*	*lonc*
p	*p, pp, b*	*prop, apparer, obs*[1]
r	*r*	*rire*
r'	*r*	*cuer*
rr	*rr*	*terra*[2]
s	*s, ss, c, ç, x*	*sap, fassa, cenat, ça, locx*
š	*ss, s, sh, h, hs*	*faissa, cais, pueysh, Foih, faihs*
t	*t, tt, d*	*tot, attenir, nud*[1]
ts	*c, z, tz, ç, gz, cz, ti*	*cel, faz, parlatz, ço, fagz, czo, fayllentia*[3]
tš	*ch, g, ich, ig, h, gz*	*chan, plag, ueich, faig, lah, gaugz*[4]
v	*u* (printed *v*)	*ven*
y	*i, y*	*gabia, preyar*
z	*s, z, ç*	*pausa, roza, riçia* (< *ridēbat*)
ž	*s, z, i*	*raso, poizo, maio*

10. The Gascon group presents certain striking divergences from the other dialects: (1) it shows a b corresponding to Provençal v, as in *be* = *ve* < *vĕnit*, *abetz* = *avetz* < *habētis*; (2) it substitutes r for l between vowels, as in *bera* = *bela* < *bĕlla*; (3) it changes initial f to h, as in *he* = *fe* < *fĭdem*. Other Gascon peculiarities are less ancient, less general, or less important.

---

[1] *G, b, d* are sounded k, p, t only at the end of a word or before a final s.

[2] Rr is generally distinguished from r, but there are a few examples of their confusion in rhyme.

[3] Ts is usually written *c* at the beginning of a word, *z* or *tz* at the end.

[4] *G* has the sound of tš only at the end of a word or combined with final *z*.

11. Some distinctions may be pointed out between the speech of the north and that of the south:—

(1) Latin ca and ga, either at the beginning of a word or after a consonant, became respectively tša and dža in the northern dialects[1], and remained unchanged in the southern: *canto > chan can*, *lŏnga > lonia longa.*

(2) Latin ct and gd became it and id in most of the north and in the southwest[1], tš and dž in most of the south and in the northwest[2]: *factum > fait fach*, *frig(i)da > freida freia.* Nct became int, nt, n′, ntš in different regions: *sanctum > saint sant sanh sanch.* Cs (Latin *x*) had various local developments—is, itš, tš—somewhat similar to those of ct: *exīre > eissir eichir ichir.*

(3) Latin d between vowels disappeared in some spots in the north and northeast[1], and became z nearly everywhere else: *audīre > auir auzir.*

(4) Latin ll became l′ in some parts of the south[2], and usually l in other regions: *bĕlla > belha bela.*

(5) Provençal final ns remains in the southeast and east, and is elsewhere generally reduced to s: *bŏnus > bons bos.* Provençal final n also falls in a large region, but its history is more intricate; the poets use indifferently forms with and without *n*: *bĕne > ben be.*

12. Several Latin consonants, when combined with a following e̯ or i̯, give results that are widely different in various localities, but the geographical distribution of the respective forms is complicated and not always clear: *pŏdium > puech poi*; *basiare > baisar basar baiiar baiar*; *bassiare > baissar baichar bachar*; *potiōnem > poizon pozon poio.* The same thing

---

[1] Cf. French. [2] Cf. Spanish.

may be said of intervocalic y (Latin *j*): *major*>*mager maier*. Also of intervocalic c, sc, g, ŋg, followed by e or i: *placēre*> *plazer plaizer plager*, *nascere*>*naisser nasser naicher nacher*, *lēgem*>*lei leg*, *ŭngere*>*onher onger*.

13. In the development of unstressed vowels there are very numerous local variations, which will be discussed later. Even among accented vowels there are some divergences:—

(1) Provençal ą, ę, ǫ before nasals become ạ, ẹ, ọ in some dialects, especially in those belonging to or bordering on the Limousin group: *canem*>cąn cạn, *vĕnit*>vęn vẹn, *bŏnum*> bǫn bọn. The poets nearly always use the forms with close vowels.

(2) The breaking of ę, ǫ, under certain conditions, into diphthongs is not common to the whole territory, and the resulting forms show local differences: *mĕum*>męu mięu, *fŏcum*>fǫc fuǫc fuęc füc. Breaking is least common in the southwest.

II. PHONOLOGY.

14. Inasmuch as Provençal, like the other Romance languages, grew out of the Latin commonly spoken under the Roman Empire, we must take this latter language as our starting-point. The transformation was so gradual and continuous that we cannot assign any date at which speech ceases to be Latin and begins to be Provençal; since, however, the various Latin dialects—destined to become later the various Romance languages—began to diverge widely in the 6th and 7th centuries, we may, for the sake of convenience, say that the Latin period ends at about this time. Before this, certain changes (which affected all the Romance tongues) had occurred in the popular language, differentiating it considerably from the classic Latin of the Augustan writers. Although the most important of these alterations have to do with inflections rather than with pronunciation, the sound-changes in Vulgar Latin are by no means insignificant.

15. It is essential at the outset to distinguish "popular" from "learned" words. The former, having always been a part of the spoken vocabulary, have been subject to the operation of all the phonetic laws that have governed the development of the language. The latter class, consisting of words borrowed by clerks, at various periods, from Latin books and from the Latin of the Church, is naturally exempt from sound-changes that occurred in the vulgar tongue before

the time of their adoption. The form of learned words depends, in the first place, on the clerical pronunciation of Latin at the date of their borrowing; then, if they came into general use, their form was subject to the influence of any phonetic laws that were subsequently in force. The fate of borrowed terms differs, therefore, according to the time of their introduction and the degree of popularity which they afterwards attained.

1. ACCENT.

16. The place of the *primary* accent, which in Classic Latin was determined by quantity, remained unchanged in Vulgar Latin even after quantitative distinctions were lost. A short vowel before a mute followed by a liquid may, in Classic Latin, be stressed or unstressed; in Vulgar Latin it is usually stressed: *cathédra*, *tenébræ*.[1]

There are some exceptions to the rule of the persistence of the accent in Vulgar Latin:—

1. An accented e or i immediately followed by the vowel of the penult transfers the stress to this latter vowel, and is itself changed to y: *filíŏlus* > *filyólus*, *mulíĕrem* > *mulyére*. This shift is perhaps due to a tendency to stress the more sonorous of two contiguous vowels.

2. An accented u immediately followed by the vowel of the penult transfers the stress to the *preceding* syllable, and is itself changed to w: *habúĕrunt* > *ábwerunt*, *tenúĕram* > *ténwera*. This shift cannot be explained on the same principle as the foregoing one; it is perhaps due in every case to analogy—*hábuit*, *ténui*, for instance, being responsible for the change in *habúerunt*, *tenúeram*.

3. Verbs compounded with a prefix, if their constituent parts were fully recognized, were usually replaced in Vulgar Latin by a formation in which the vowel and the accent of the simple verb were preserved: *défĭcit* > *disfácit*, *réddĭdi* > *reddédi*, *rénĕgo* > *renégo*, *réquĭrit* > *requærit*. In

[1] For some exceptions see *Rom.*, XXXII, 591; P. Marchot, *Phon.*, p. 9.

rĕ́cĭpit > *recípit* the accent but not the vowel was restored, speakers having ceased to associate this verb with *capio.* In *cóllĭgo*, *ĕ́rĭgo*, *ĕ́xĕo*, *ínflo* the composite nature of the word was apparently not recognized.

4. The adverbs *ĭ́llāc*, *ĭ́llīc* accented their last syllable, by the analogy of *hāc*, *hīc*.

17. In Provençal the primary accent falls on the same syllable as in Vulgar Latin: *bonitātem* > V. L. *bonitáte* > Pr. *bontát*, *compŭtum* > V. L. *cómputu* > Pr. *cónte*; *cathĕdra* > V. L. *catḗdra* > Pr. *cadḗira*; *filiŏlus* > V. L. *filyólus* > Pr. *filhṓls*, *tenuĕram* > V. L. *ténwera* > Pr. *téngra*, *requĭrit* > V. L. *requærit* > Pr. *requér*, *illac* > V. L. *illác* > Pr. *lai.*

1. Some learned words have an irregular accentuation, apparently due to a mispronunciation of the Latin: *cándĭdum* > *quandí*, *grammátĭca* > *gramatíca*, *láchrÿmo* > *lagrím*, *spírĭtum* > *esprít* (perhaps from the formula *spirítui sancto*). Others were adopted with the correct stress, but shifted it later: *fábrĭca* > *fábrega* > *fabréga* (and *fárga*), *fémĭna* > *fémena* > *feména* (and *fémna*), *láchrÿma* > *lágrema* > *lagréma*, *sémĭnat* > *sémena* > *seména* (and *sémna*), *vírgĭnem* > *vérgena* > *vergína* (and *vérge*).

2. *Dimércres* < *dīe Mercūrī* has evidently been influenced by *divénres* < *dīe Vĕnĕris.*

3. Some irregularities due to inflection will be discussed under Morphology.

18. The *secondary* accent, in Vulgar Latin, seems not to have followed the Classic Latin quantitative rule, but to have fallen regularly on the second syllable from the primary stress: *cŏ́gĭtó*, *cupĭ̀dĭtā́tem.* If this secondary accent *followed* the tonic, its vowel probably developed as an unstressed post-tonic vowel; if it *preceded*, its vowel was apparently treated as a stressed vowel. This treatment was doubtless continued in Provençal until the intertonic vowel dropped out: *cógĭtó cógĭtánt* > *cug cúian* (cf. *cánto cántant* > *can cántan*), *cupĭ̀dĭtā́tem* > *cupéðitáte* > *cubéðtát* > *cobeitát.* As may be seen from this last example, after the fall of the intertonic vowel, the secondary stress, being brought next to the primary, disappeared, and its vowel was henceforth unaccented. Cf. § 45, 1.

19. Short, unemphatic words had no accent in Vulgar Latin, and were attached as particles to the beginning or the end of another word: *te vídet, áma me.* Such words, if they were not monosyllabic, tended to become so; a dissyllabic proclitic beginning with a vowel regularly, in Vulgar Latin, lost its first syllable: *illum vídeo* > V. L. *lu véyo* > Pr. *lo vei.* A word which was used sometimes independently, sometimes as a particle, naturally developed double forms.

2. VOWELS.

QUANTITY.

20. Latin had the following vowels, which might be long or short: a, e, i, o, u. The diphthongs, æ, œ, au, eu, ui, were always long: æ and œ, however, were simplified into monophthongs, mainly in the Republican epoch, *æ* being sounded ę̄, *œ* probably ẹ̄; au retained (save in some popular dialects) its old pronunciation; eu did not occur in any word that survived; ui, in *cui, illui,* in Vulgar Latin, was accented *úi* (as in *fui*). The simple vowels, except a, were, doubtless from early times, slightly different in quality according to their quantity, the long vowels being sounded close, the short open: ẹ̄, ị̄, ọ̄, ụ̄; ę̆, į̆, ǫ̆, ų̆.

21. Between the 1st and the 7th century of our era, the Classic Latin quantity died out: it had apparently disappeared from unstressed vowels as early as the 4th century, from stressed by the 6th. It left its traces, however, as we have seen, upon accentuation (§ 16), and also upon vowel quality, the originally long and short remaining differentiated in sound, if they were accented. Of the unaccented vowels, only i shows sure signs of such a differentiation, and even for i the distinction is evident only in a final syllable: *vēnī vēnĭt* > vẹnị vẹni̮t.

ACCENTED VOWELS.

22. The vowels of Vulgar Latin are a, ẹ, e̮, ị, i̮, ọ, o̮, ụ, u̮, with the diphthongs áu and úi; the old æ and œ had become identical in sound with e̮ and ẹ. As early as the 3d century of our era, i̮ was changed, in nearly all the Empire, to ẹ, and thus became identical with the vowel coming from original ē. A little later, perhaps, u̮, in the greater part of the Empire, became ọ, thus coinciding with the vowel that was originally ō. Ypsilon, in words taken from the Greek, was identified, in early borrowings, with Latin u; in later ones, with Latin i: *βύρσα* > Pr. *borsa*, *γῦρος* > Pr. *girs*. Omicron, which apparently had the close sound in Greek, generally (but not always) retained it in recently borrowed words in Vulgar Latin: *τόρνος* > tọrnus (cf. Pr. tọrn), but *κόλαφος* > *cŏlăphus* = cọlapus or co̮lapus (cf. Pr. co̮lp).

The development of the Vulgar Latin vowels in Provençal will now be examined in detail:—

a

23. Cl. L. ā, ă > V. L. a > Pr. a̮: *ărbŏrem* > a̮rbre, *grātum* > gra̮t, *măre* > ma̮r.

1. The ending *-arius* shows an irregular development in French and Provençal, the Provençal forms being mainly such as would come from *-ĕrius*; as in *parlier*, *parleira*. In the earliest stage we find apparently -e̮r′ and -e̮r′a; then -e̮r′ and -e̮ir′a; next -e̮r, -ie̮r and -e̮ira, -ie̮ira; finally, with a reciprocal influence of the two genders, -e̮r, -ie̮r, -e̮ir, and -e̮ra, -ie̮ra, -e̮ira, -ie̮ira: *caballarium* > *c*(*h*)*avaler -ier*, *-eir*, **man*(*u*)*aria*

>*manera -iera -eira -ieira*. The peculiar treatment of this suffix has not been satisfactorily explained. See E. R. Zimmermann, *Die Geschichte des lateinischen Suffixes -arius in den romanischen Sprachen*, 1895; E. Staaff, *Le suffixe -arius dans les langues romanes*, Upsala, 1896, reviewed by Marchot in *Zs.*, XXI, 296, by Körting in *Zeitschrift für französische Sprache*, XXII, 55; Meyer-Lübke, *Gram.*, I, 222, § 237; Zimmermann in *Zs.*, XXVI, 591; Thomas in *Rom.*, XXXI, 481. The most promising theory is that of Thomas: that *-arius* was associated with the Germanic ending *-ari* and participated in the *umlaut* which affected the latter; cf. also P. Marchot, *Phon.*, pp. 34–36.

2. In Gascony and Languedoc *ei* is used for *ai* <*habeo*. The *ei* perhaps developed first as a future ending (*amar -ei*) by analogy of the preterit ending *-ei* (*amei*): see Morphology, §§ 152, 1, 162, (4), 175, (4), where this latter ending is discussed also. For a different explanation, see Meyer-Lübke, *Gram.*, I, 222, § 237.

3. A few apparent irregularities are to be traced to the vocabulary of Vulgar Latin. For instance, Pr. *sereisa* represents, not Cl. L. *cĕrăsus*, but V. L. *cĕrĕsĕa*: see Meyer-Lübke, *Einf.*, § 103. *Uebre* is from **ŏpĕrit*, or *apĕrit* modified by **cŏpĕrit* = *cōperit*. *Voig* is from **vŏcĭtum* = *vacuum*: *Einf.*, § 114.

4. Such forms as *fontaina* = *fontana* <*fontāna*, etc., and *tres* = *tras* < *trans*, etc., are French or belong to the borderland between French and Provençal.

24. In some dialects, particularly in Rouergue, Limousin, Auvergne, and Dauphiné, a became ạ before a nasal, and at the end of a monosyllable or an oxytone: *cánem* > cạn, *grandem* > grạnt, *cadit* > cạ, *stat* > estạ.

1. The conditions differ somewhat in the various dialects, according as the nasal consonant falls or remains, and is followed by another consonant or not. In Limousin the sound is ạ before an n that cannot fall: see § 11, (5). In Rouergue and in Dauphiné, ạ appears before all nasals. The poets generally follow the Limousin usage. See F. Pfützner, *Ueber die Aussprache des provenzalischen A*, Halle, 1884.

ẹ

25. Cl. L. ē, ĭ, œ > V. L. ẹ > Pr. ẹ: *habēre* > avẹr, *mē* > mẹ, *mensem* > mẹs, *plēnum* > plẹn, *rēgem* > rẹi, *vēndĕre* > vẹndre; *ĭnter* > ẹntre, *fĭdem* > fẹ, *malĭtia* > malẹza, *mĭnus* > mẹns, *mĭttĕre* > mẹtre, *sĭccum* > sẹc, *vĭrĭdem* > vẹrt; *pœna* > pẹna.

1. Some words have ę instead of ẹ:—

(*a*) The ending *-ētis* in the present indicative becomes -ętz through the analogy of ętz < *ĕstis*.

(*b*) Camęl (also ẹ), candęla (also ẹ), cruzęl, fizęl (also ẹ), maissęla have ę through the analogy of the suffix -ęl < *-ĕllus*. In *camel* the substitution probably goes back to Vulgar Latin.

(*c*) Many learned words, including proper names, have ę for ẹ: decręt, Elizabęt, Moysęs, pantęra, requięs, secręt (ẹ), sencęr.

(*d*) Espęr for espẹr < *spēro*, quęt for quẹt < *qu(i)ētum* are perhaps bad rhymes. Bartolomeo Zorzi, a Venetian, rhymes -ẹs with -ęs; in Catalan these two endings were not distinguished.

(*e*) Individual cases: adęs, 'at once,' probably from *ad id ĭpsum*, seems to have been affected by pręs and apręs < *ad prĕssum*; mostięr < *monastērium* shows the influence of *ministĕrium*; nẹr nięr (also nẹr nęgre) < *nĭgrum* perhaps shows the influence of entęr entięr and the numerous adjectives in -ęr -ięr; nęu nięu nęy < *nĭvem* has been attracted by bręu gręu, lęu; sęze < *sēdĕcim* follows sęis < *sĕx*; senęstre (cf. late Lat. *sinexter*) is evidently influenced by dęstre.

2. Many words have i instead of ẹ:—

(*a*) *Berbitz* = *vervēcem*, *camisa* = *camĭsia*, *dit* = *dĭgĭtum* come from alternative V. L. forms, *berbīcem*, **camīsia*, **dīgitum*.

(*b*) In many learned words Latin ĭ is represented by i in Provençal: *albir*, *martire*, *edifici*, *iuzizi*, *servizi*, *vici*, etc.; *iusticia*, *leticia*, *tristicia*, etc.; *planissa*, *sebissa*, etc. *Aurilha* (also ẹ) < *aurĭcula*, *cilh* (also *cieilh*, *sobreselhs*) < *cĭlium*, *issilh* < *exĭlium*, *familha* < *famĭlia*, *maistre* (also maẹstre maiẹstre) < *magĭstrum*, *meravilha* (also ẹ) < *mirabĭlia*, *perilh* < *perĭculum*, etc., are probably learned forms. *Máistre* and *mestre* are French.

(*c*) *Ciri* (*cere*) = *cēreum*, *iure* (cf. *ebriac*) = *ēbrium* (or **ĕbrium*), *marquis* (ẹ), *merci* (ẹ), *país* (ẹ) = **pagēnsem*, *plazir* (ẹ), *pris* (ẹ), etc., are French. For a discussion of *iure* and a different explanation of *ciri*, see P. Savj-Lopez, *Dell' "Umlaut" provenzale*, 1902, p. 4.

(*d*) *Ins* (also *entz*) < *ĭntus*, *dins* (also *dens*) < *de ĭntus*, *dintre* (cf. *en*, *entre*) < *de ĭnter* have not been satisfactorily explained. Regular forms with ẹ are found in Béarn, Gascony, Dauphiné, and the Alps.

(*e*) Individual cases: *tapit* < *ταπήτιον* shows the modern pronunciation of Greek *η*; *verin* = *venēnum* is an example of substitution of suffix.

3. *Arnei*, *fei*, *mei* = *me*, *palafrei*, *perquei*, *sei* = *se* are French or borderland forms. *Mercey*, *rey* = *re*, used by Marcabru, seem to be due either to an imitation of such forms as the preceding or to the analogy of *crei cre* < *crēdo*. Cf. § 65, N, 3.

4. *Contránher* seems to be a fusion of *constrĭngere* and *contrahere*; *vendanha* < *vindēmia* shows French influence.

26. An ẹ in hiatus became i: *lĭgat* > lia, **sĭam* > sia, *vĭa* > via.

27. When there was in the next syllable a final ī, V. L. ẹ was changed in Provençal to i: *ecc'ĭllī* > cilh, *ecc'ĭstī* > cist, *fēcī* > fis, **prēsī* > pris, **vēnuī* > vinc, *vigĭntī* **vĭntī* > vint.

1. In the nominative plural of masculine nouns and adjectives this change was regularly prevented by the analogy of the singular and the accusative plural: *mĭssī* > *mes*, *plēnī* > *plen*. We find, however, *cabil* < *capĭllī*.

2. *Dec* for **dic* < *dēbuī* is probably due to the influence of the weak ending -ẹc, which owes its ẹ to the -ẹi -ẹst -ẹt of the first and third conjugations. *Venguest* for *venguist* < **venuĭstī* is due both to the influence of the plural forms *venguem*, *venguetz* and to the analogy of the weak preterits, such as *cantest*, *vendest*.

ę

28. Cl. L. ĕ, æ > V. L. ę > Pr. ę: *infĕrnum* > enfęrn, *fĕrrum* > fęr, *pĕdem* > pę, *trĕmŭlat* > tręmbla; *cælum* > cęl, *quærit* > quęr.

1. Such forms as *glisia*, *lire*, *pire*, *pis*, *profit* are French. *Profich* may be a cross between *profieg* and *profit*, or it may be due to the analogy of *dich*.

2. *Cossint*, *mint*, *sint*, used by Arnaut Daniel, are perhaps faulty rhymes.

3. *Auzil* < *avicĕllī*, in the *Boeci*, may be due to the analogy of such plural forms as *cabil* < *capĭllī*, *il* < *ĭllī*, etc. *Briu*, sometimes used for

breu < *brĕvem*, is evidently connected with *abrivar*, 'hasten,' the origin of which is uncertain. *Elig* shows the influence either of *eligir* (beside *elegir*) or of *dig*. *Ginh* = *genh* < *ingĕnium* evidently follows *ginhos* < *ingeniōsus* and its derivatives. *Isme* (*esme*) is a post-verbal noun from **ismar* (cf. *azismamen*), a dialect form of *esmar* < *æstimare*. *Quis* < **quæsi*, *tinc* < *tĕnui* are due to the analogy of *pris* < **prēsī*, *vinc* < **vēnui*.

4. Beside nęula < *nĕbula*, we find *nebla*, *neble*, presumably from the same source, and also *nible*, *niól*, *nióla*, *niúl*, *niúla*, *nivól*. According to Nigra, *Archivio glottologico italiano*, XV, 494, *nūbes* > *nūbĭlus* > **nībŭlus* (and **nībūlus*?), whence might be derived **níŭlus* **niúlus*, which would account for *niól–a*, *niúl–a*, and perhaps for a **nívol* > *nivól*. *Nible* might be regarded as a cross between *neble* and *niul*.

5. In ęs < *ĕst* the ę probably comes from such combinations as mę's, quę's, understood as m'ęs, qu'ęs. Espęlh < *spĕculum* shows the influence of cossęlh, solęlh. Estęla presupposes a Latin **stēla* or **stēlla* for stēlla: cf. the Fr. and It.

6. *Plais*, 'hedge' seems to be a cross between *plĕxus* and *paxillus*, 'fence.' *Vianda* (< *vivenda*?) is probably French.

7. *Volon* < *volentem* shows the influence of the ending *-ŭndus*.

8. *Greuga* < *con-gregar* has been influenced by *greu* < **grĕvem* = *gravem* influenced by *lĕvem*. Cf. *grey* < *grĕgem*.

29. Before a nasal, in most of the dialects of Limousin, Languedoc, and Gascony, ę became ẹ: *bĕne* > bẹn, *dicĕntem* > dizẹn, *tĕmpus* > tẹms, *tĕnet* > tẹn, *vĕniam* > vẹnha, *vĕntum* > vẹnt.

30. Early in the history of Provençal, before u, i, or one of the palatal consonants l′, r′, s′, z′, y, tš, dž, an ę broke into ię, except in a few dialects of the west and north: *dĕus* > dięus, *mĕum* > mięu; *amāvi* > **amai* > amęi amięi, **fĕria* > fięira, **ec*(*c*)*lĕsia*? (Cf. *Zs.*, XXV, 344) > glięiza, *lĕctum* > lięit, *pĕjus* > pięis; *vĕtŭlum* *vĕclum* > vięlh, *ministĕrium* > mestięr, **ec*(*c*)*lĕsia*? > glięza, *mĕdia* > mięia, *lĕctum* > lięg. There seems to be also, at least in some dialects, a tendency to break the ę before a g or a k: *lĕgunt* > lięgon; **sĕquit* > sęc sięc, subjunctive sięgas (sęga), but infinitive sęgre < * *sĕquere*.[1]

The breaking was probably due to a premature lifting of the tongue under the influence of a following high vowel or a palatal (or velar) consonant.[2] Before u it occurred everywhere except in the extreme west; before palatals the ę apparently remained intact both in the extreme west and in Quercy, Rouergue, Auvergne, and Dauphiné. At first, no doubt, the diphthong was less marked than it became in the 12th and 13th centuries. It is not indicated in our oldest text, the *Boeci* (*breu*, *deu*, *eu*, *mei*, *meler*, *vel*)[3], and it frequently remains unexpressed even in the writings of the literary period.

It is to be noted that ę does not break before u < l nor before i < ð: *bĕllus* > bęls > bęus, *pĕtra* > * pęðra > pęira, *Pĕtrum* > * Pęðre > Pęire, *rĕtro* > * ręðre > ręire[4]. The breaking must, therefore, have occurred before these developments of l and ð, both of which apparently antedate the *Boeci*: cf. *euz* = *els*, v. 139; *eu* = *el*, v. 155; *Teiric* < * *Teðric* < *Theodorīcum*, v. 44, etc. On the other hand, there is no diphthong before ts, dz, s, z coming from Latin c′, cy, pty, tty, ty: *dĕcem* > dętz, *pĕttia* (or *pĕcia*) > pęssa, *nĕptia* > nęssa, * *prĕtiat* > pręza, *prĕtium* > prętz[5]. The breaking, therefore, took

---

[1] There is no diphthong in the preterit ending -ęc: cazęc, etc.

[2] This view is a modification of the theory developed by C. Voretzsch in his admirable treatise, *Zur Geschichte der Diphthongierung im Altprovenzalischen*, Halle, 1900. That ę is not affected by an i in the following syllable is shown by such words as empęri, evangęli, saltęri, which must have been adopted fairly early. The same thing is true of ǫ: apostǫli, ǫli, etc.

[3] The diphthong of ǫ occurs, however, in this text, v. 203, in *uel* < *ŏculi*.

[4] *Derrier* (*derer*, *dereer*), beside *dereire*, is manifestly due to the influence of *primier*. To the influence of the same ending *-ier*, as in *carr*(*i*)*eira*, is to be ascribed the diphthong in *cad*(*i*)*eira* < *cathĕdra*.

[5] The things just said of ę are true of ǫ: there is no breaking before u < l (tǫut = tǫlt) nor before ts, dz, s, z (*nŏcet* > nǫtz, * *nŏptias* > nǫssas).

place after these consonants had ceased to be palatal. We may ascribe it with some confidence to the period between the seventh and tenth centuries.

1. A number of cases of ię before r are doubtless to be explained by analogy. *Hĕri* > ęr; *autre* + *er* > autręr, which, through the influence of adjectives in –ęr –ięr, became autrięr: hence the form ięr. *Fĕrio*, *mĕreo* > fięr, mięr; hence, by analogy, the first person forms profięr, quięr, then the third person forms fięr, mięr, profięr, quięr, sięrf (but sęrvon, sęrva), and the subjunctives ofięira, sofię(i)ra.

2. Ięsc (= *ĕxeo*), ięscon, ięsca receive their diphthong either from earlier forms with s′ or from ięis < *ĕxit*.

ị

31. Cl. L. ī > V. L. ị: *amīcum* > amịc, *fīnem* > fịn, *trīstem* > trịst.

1. Fręg, fręit are from V. L. **frĭgdum* = *frīgĭdum*, the ĭ being perhaps due to the analogy of *rĭgĭdum*.

32. In the 13th century or earlier the group iu, in most dialects, became ieu: *captīvum* > caitiu caitieu, *æstīvum* > estiu esticu, *revīvĕre* > reviure revieure, *sī vōs* > sius sieus.

ọ

33. Cl. L. ō, ŭ > V. L. ọ > Pr. ọ, which developed into ụ probably during the literary period: *dolōrem* > dolọr, *spōnsa* > espọsa, *flōrem* > flọr; *bŭcca* > bọca, *gŭla* > gọla.

1. An irregular ǫ, which is found in some words, goes back to Vulgar Latin: cǫbra = *re–cŭperat*, cǫsta (also ọ) = *cōnstat*, nǫra = *nŭra*, ǫu = *ōvum*, plǫia = *plŭvia*, redǫbla = **redŭplat*, sǫbra = *sŭperat*, suefre = *sŭffero*. V. L. **cŏperat* may be regarded as a fusion of *cŭperat* and **cŏperit* (§ 40, 1; cf. *Rom.* XXXI, 9); **cŏstat* is unexplained; **nŏra* shows the influence of *sŏror* and *sŏcĕra*; the *ŏ* of **ŏvum* has been explained as due to differentiation from the following *v*; **plŏia* is to be connected with the popular *plŏvĕre* (cf. Meyer-Lübke, *Einf.*, § 142); **sŏperat* follows the analogy of **cŏperat*; **sŏffero* evidently follows *ŏffero*. Redǫbla (also ọ)

is not accounted for. If trǫba has anything to do with *tŭrbat*, it was perhaps influenced by *prŏbat* (cf. *Zs.*, XXVIII, 50).

2. Some words have ü: iüs (also iọs) < *deōrsum* shows the influence of süs < *sūrsum*; lür (usually lọr) < *illōrum* (cf. *lur* in the dialects of Navarre and Aragon) comes through an **illūrum* due to the analogy of *illūi* = *illi*; melhüra (ọ), peiüra (ọ) perhaps follow aüra < **a(u)gūrat*; rancüra is a mixture of *rancōrem* and *cūra*; üis is from V. L. *ūstium* = *ōstium* (cf. *Zs.*, XXV, 355); üpa < *ŭpŭpa* is due to onomatopœa.

3. The adverbs *ar*, *ara*, *er*, *era*, *eras*, meaning 'now,' are hardly to be connected with *hōra*. Meyer-Lübke takes *era*, etc., from a Latin **era* corresponding to Greek ἄρα; *ara*, *ar* may come directly from ἄρα, ἄρ: cf. *Gr.*, III, 552, note.

4. *Adoutz*, 'fount,' from *addŭctus*, probably owes its *ou* to the analogy of *doutz*, *adouzar*, from *dŭlcis*.

5. *Tonleu*, 'tariff,' from τελώνιον, shows a metathesis of vowels and of consonants.

34. Before tš, dž (and it, id), before n', and before final i, an ọ becomes ü in various dialects: *cōgĭtat* > cüia cüida, **stŭdiat* > estüia, *fŭgit* > füg, *refŭgium* > refüg; *jŭngĕre* > iünher, *ŭngĕre* > ünher, *pŭgnum* > pünh; *dŭī* > düi, *sŭm* > sọ + i > süi. The ü before tš, dž apparently occurs everywhere except in Dauphiné; before n' it is to be found in nearly all the dialects of the north and west; before final i it seems to be limited to Bordeaux, Auvergne, and a part of Languedoc.

ǫ

35. Cl. L. ŏ > V. L. ǫ > Pr. ǫ: *cŏr* > cǫr, *cŏrpus* > cǫrs, *mŏrtem* > mǫrt, *ŏpĕra* > ǫbra, *rŏta* > rǫda.

1. For demọra (also ǫ) < *demŏrat, see Meyer-Lükbe, *Gram.*, I, 204, § 220. For prǫa (also prǫa, prueva) < *prŏbat*, see *Rom.*, XXXI, 10, footnote 3.

36. Before a nasal, in most of the dialects of Limousin, Languedoc, and Gascony, ǫ became ọ: *bŏnum* > bọn, *fŏntem*

>fo̩nt, *pŏntem*>po̩nt. Cf. E. Levy in *Mélanges de philologie romane dédiés à Carl Wahlund*, 1896, p. 207.

1. If the nasal was n′, the vowel remained open in most or all of these dialects: *cŏgnĭta*>*coinda cuenda cuenhda*, *lŏnge*>*lonh luenh*, *sŏmnium*>*sonh suenh*.

37. Early in the history of Provençal, before u, a labial consonant, a g or a k, an i, or one of the palatal consonants l′, n′, r′, s′, z′, y, tš, dž, an o̩ broke, in most dialects, into a diphthong which developed into ue, üo, üe, or ü[1]: *bŏvem*> bo̩u büo̩u büeu, **ŏvum*> o̩u üou üeu, *nŏvus*> no̩us nüous nüeus; **cŏpero*>co̩bri cüebre[2], *nŏva*>no̩va nüeva, *ŏpus*> o̩ps üops, *prŏbat*>pro̩a prüeva, **trŏpo*?>tro̩p trüeb; *cŏquus* >co̩cs cüocs cüex, *fŏcum*>fo̩c füoc füec füc, *crŏcus*>gro̩cs grüocs grüecs, *jŏcum*>io̩c iüoc iüec iüc, *lŏcus*>lo̩cs lüocs lüecs, *lŏcat*>lüoga, *pŏtui*>püec, *sŏc(ĕ)rum*> (so̩zer) so̩gre süegre (fem. süegra); **ingrŏssiat*>engro̩issa engrüeissa, **angŏstia*>engo̩issa engüeissa, *nŏctem*>no̩it nüoit nüeit, *ŏcto*> o̩it üeit, *pŏstea*>po̩issas püeissas, *prŏximus*>pro̩ymes prüeymes; *fŏlia*>fo̩lha füolha füelha fülha, *ŏcŭlus ŏclus*>o̩lhs üolhs üelhs ülhs, *lŏnge*>lo̩nh lüenh, *sŏmnium*>so̩nh süenh, *cŏrium*>co̩r cüer, *pŏstea*>pües, *prŏximum*>pro̩sme prüesme, **plŏia*>plo̩ia plüeia plüia, **inŏdiat*>eno̩ia enüeia enüia, **pŏdiat*>po̩ia püeia püia, *nŏctem*>nüoch nüech nüh, *ŏcto*> üeg.

The breaking was probably due to a premature lifting of the tongue under the influence of a following high vowel or a palatal or velar consonant, or to a premature partial closure

[1] The conditions are not quite the same as for e: an e̩ does not break before a labial (ne̩ps) nor before n′ (ve̩nha). Breaking before g and k seems more general for o̩ than for e̩.

[2] So the second person forms *cuebres*, *uebres*, *uefres*, and the third person forms *cuebre*, *uebre*, *uefre*; cf. co̩bron, o̩bri, etc.

of the lips in anticipation of a following labial. Before i or a palatal the diphthong was at the start presumably üo; before u or a labial or velar consonant, uo: from these two types, the first of which influenced the second, came the later developments. Ü is a reduction of üo or üe; it apparently does not occur before u.

The dialect conditions are mixed, the development in each region depending somewhat on the following sound. In the southwest, ǫ and ue seem to prevail; in the northwest, ü; in the west, in Limousin, and in Auvergne, üe; in Languedoc, üo; in the east and south, üe, üo, ǫ.

The date of breaking is discussed in § 30.

1. In some words where a diphthong would be expected, none is found, although it may have existed: mǫu < _mŏvet_, nǫu < _nŏvem_, plǫu < *_plŏvit_; trǫp < _prop_; brǫcs < *_brŏccus_, iǫgon < _jŏcunt_, lǫgui < _lŏco_. The form püoc or püec < _pŏtui_ is regularly reserved for the first person, _pŏtuit_ being represented by pǫc.

2. A few cases of irregular breaking are easily explained: püosc püesc (= _pŏssum_) and püosca püesca (= _pŏssim_) owe their diphthong either to earlier forms with s′ or to the analogy of püec; sǫfre süefre süfre (= _sŭfſert_) are from *_sŏfferit_, formed upon *_ŏfferit_ = _ŏffert_ (cf. § 33, 1); vüelc (= _vŏlui_) follows the analogy of vüelh (< *_vŏleo_ = _vŏlo_) and of püec.

ụ

38. Cl. L. ū > V. L. ụ > Pr. ü: *_habūtus_ > avütz, _jūstum_ > iüst, _mūrum_ > mür, _mūtus_ > mütz, _nūdus_ > nütz, _plūs_ > plüs.

The date of the change of ụ into ü is not known; there is no ü in Catalan, and there may have been none in early Gascon. It seems likely that the Celts, when they adopted Latin, pronounced ū a little further forward in the mouth than did the Romans; that their ụ continued to advance gradually toward the front of the mouth until it became ü; and that this ü spread to the parts of France that were not originally Celtic.[1] In the literary period the sound was probably ü in the Provençal region, with the possible exception of Gascony.

1. Pr. ǫnze represents a V. L. **ŭndĕcim*, which in Gaul and Spain replaced *ūndĕcim*. Lǫita lücha, trǫcha trücha probably go back to Latin double forms, **lŭcta lūcta*, **trŭcta trūcta*. Engǫissa < V. L. **angŏstia* = *angūstia* (cf. Italian *angoscia*).

2. Nǫssas < **nŏptias* = *nūptias*, by analogy of **nŏvius*, 'bridegroom,' from *nŏvus*.

au

39. Cl. L. au > V. L. au > Pr. au: *aurum* > aur, *gaudium* > gaug, *paucum* > pauc, *thesaurus* > tesaurs.

1. *Bloi* < *blauþr*, *ioi*, *ioia*, *ioios*, *lotia* < **laubja*, *noiza*, *onta* < *hauniþa*, *or*, *sor*, *tesor*, etc., are French. *Iai*, 'joy,' seems to be a fusion of *ioi* and Pr. *iai* = *gai*.

2. *Anta* < *hauniþa* is unexplained.

UNACCENTED VOWELS.

40. (1) The fate of an unaccented vowel depended largely upon the syllable in which it stood: in general, unstressed vowels in the initial syllable remained intact, while all vowels, except a, fell (at different dates) in the other syllables. The fall of unaccented vowels resulted in many new consonant groups: *collocáre* > colcár, *hóminem* > ómne, *sábbatum* > sápte.

(2) The vowels ẹ̯ and i̯, instead of falling or remaining unchanged, became y in Vulgar Latin, early in our era: *alea* > alya, *diŭrnus* > dyụrnus, *mĕdium* > mẹdyu. Similarly u̯ became w: *placui* > placwi, *tĕnuis* > tẹnwis.

1. Apparently, however, ẹ̯é, i̯é > e; ọ̯ó, u̯ó > o: *prĕhĕndĕre* > *prĕndĕre*; *abĭĕtem* > **abētem*, *facĭēbat* > **facēbat*, *parĭĕtem* > *parētem*, *quĭētus* >

[1] For a discussion of the date, see K. Nyrop, *Grammaire historique de la langue française* (Copenhagen, 1899–1903), I, § 187.

quĕtus; *cŏhŏrtem* > *cōrtem*, *cŏŏpĕrit* > *cōpĕrit* **cŏpĕrit*; *dŭŏdĕcim* > **dōdĕcim*. The short e and o in *prĕndĕre* and **cŏpĕrit* are not accounted for. In *mulĭĕrem*[1] > Pr. molhẹr the i̯ remained long enough (perhaps under the influence of the nominative *mŭlier*) to palatalize the l.

INITIAL SYLLABLE.

41. Usually, in the literary language, Latin a > Pr. a; Latin æ, œ, and e, i (without regard to quantity) > Pr. e; Latin o, u (long or short) > Pr. o; Lat. au > Pr. au, unless the next syllable contained an ú, in which case the au was reduced (in the Vulgar Latin time) to a. Ex.: *amīcum* > amic, *caballus* > cavals; *æquālem* > egal, **pœnĭtēre* > penẹdre, *dēbēre* > devẹr, *mĕliōrem* > melhọr, *dīlēctum* > delẹit, *dīvīnum* > devin, *dīvīdĕre* > devire, *fīnīre* > fenir, *mĭnōrem* > menọr; *plōrāre* > plorar, *sōlātium* > solatz, *cŏlōrem* > colọr, **vŏlēre* > volẹr, *mūstēla* > mostẹla, *sŭbĭnde* > sovẹn; *aucĕllum* > auzẹl, *audīre* > auzir, *augŭstum* > aọst, **augūrium* > aür.

1. An initial vowel is occasionally lost, either through elision with the article (**eclĕsia* > *eglẹisa, la eglẹisa > la glẹisa) or through the dropping of a prefix (*ingĕnium* > engẹnh gẹnh): *epĭscŏpus* > *bisbes*, *alauda* > *lauzeta*, *occasiōnem* > *ocaiso caiso*.

2. In a few words the vowel of the initial syllable disappeared, for some unknown reason, in Vulgar Latin: **cŏrrŏtŭlāre* > **crŏtŭlāre* > *crollar*, *dīrēctus* > *drēctus*[2] > *dreitz*, *quĭrītāre* > **crītāre* > *cridar*.

3. *Domne*, used familiarly as a proclitic (§ 19), lost its first syllable, and, before a vowel, was reduced to *n*. The combinations *de n*, *que n* (followed by a proper name) were understood as *d'en*, *qu'en*; hence the title *en*, 'Sir.' See Schultz-Gora in *Zs.*, XXVI, 588; Elise Richter in *Zs.*, XXVII, 193.

4. The proclitic ọ probably comes from a V. L. *ot*, not from *aut*.

42. The vowel of the initial syllable, especially in verbs,

[1] For the accent, see § 16, 1.

[2] Spelled *drictus*: see Schuchardt, *Vocalismus des Vulgärlateins*, II, 422.

was extremely subject to the influence of analogy: cülhir (ọ) through cülh (ọ) < *cŏllĭgit*, dizẹn < *dīcĕntem* through dire < *dīcĕre*, dürar through dür < *dūrum* and düra < *dūrat*, finir through fin < *fīnem*, fivẹla through fibla < *fībula*, puẹiar (ọ) through puẹia (ọ) < **pŏdiat*.

1. Avangẹli (e) is perhaps influenced by *avan*; blisọ (e) < *blas* may possibly have been influenced by *tiso*; gazardọ < *wiðarlôn* shows the influence of *gazanhar*; in piucẹla (pülcẹla) < **pūellicĕlla* (*Zs.*, XXV, 343) the püu of the first syllable was changed to piu perhaps under the influence of *pius* < *pius*; in *vas* = *ves* < *ve*(*r*)*sus* the a is due to the analogy of *az* < *ad*; *vais* is unexplained, *vaus* follows *daus* (§ 44, 6). If dessẹ is from *de exīn*, the first syllable is irregular. Beside *maniar* < *manducare* are unexplained forms *meniar miniar*. In *duptar* (*o*), *suritz* (*o*) the *u* doubtless represents ụ or ọ, not ü. *Girofle* < Καρυόφυλλον and *olifan orifan* < *elephantem* are French.

43. Sometimes the initial syllable was altered by a change of prefix or a false idea of etymology: aucire < *occīdĕre* (cf. the Italian and Rumanian forms), diman (e) < *de mâne* and dimẹnge < *domĭnĭcum* (cf. di < *dīem*), dementre < *dum ĭntĕrim* (cf. de < *de*), engọissa < **angŭstia* (cf. en < *in*), envanezir < *evanēscĕre*, escür < *obscūrum* (cf. es- < *ex-*), preọn prefọn (o) < *profŭndum*, redọn < *rotŭndum* (*re-* in V. L.: Schuchardt, *Vocalismus des Vulgärlateins*, II, 213), trabalh < *trepalium* (cf. tra- < *tra-* = *trans-*).

1. On the same principle are doubtless to be explained such double forms as *evori* (*a*), *saboros* (*e*), *socors* (*e*), *somondre* (*e*), *soror* (*e*). *Serori* occurs in a Latin inscription.

2. The prefix *eccu-*, under the influence of *ac* and *atque*, became **accu-* in southern Gaul and elsewhere: *aco* < **accu'hoc*, *aquel* < **accu'ĭllum*, *aquest* < **accu'ĭstum*, *aqui* < **accu'hīc*. *Eissi* < *ecce hīc* sometimes becomes *aissi* through the analogy of *aissi* < *ac sīc*.

3. In such forms as *tresanar*, the prefix *tres-* is French.

44. Local or partial phonetic changes affected the initial

syllable of many words: demandar (do–)<*demandāre*, emplir (üm–)<*implēre*; ciutat cieutat<*cīvĭtātem*; eissir issir<*exīre*, getar gitar<**jĕctāre*; crear criar<*creāre*; merce (mar–)< *mercēdem*; delgat (dal–)<*delicātum*.

1. Nearly everywhere there is a tendency to change e to o, u, or ü before a labial, especially before m: *premier promier prumier*, *remas romas*, *semblar somblar*, *trebalh trubalh*. So *de ves*>**do ves*>*dous*.

2. In the 13th century, nearly everywhere, iu>ieu: *piucela pieucela*.

3. Many dialects of the north and west change ei and e to i: *deissendre dissendre*, *eissam issam*, *eissi issi*, *eissilh issilh*, *leisso lisso*, *meitat mitat*; *degerir* (*i*), *denhar* (*i*), *disnar*, *en in*, *enfern* (*i*), *entrar* (*i*), *envers* (*i*), *escien icient*, proclitic *est ist*, *estar* (*i*), *estiers*(*i*), *Felip* (*i*), *gelos* (*i*), *genhos* (*i*), *genolh* (*i*), *gequir* (*i*), *guereiar* (*i*), *guerensa* (*i*), *i*(*n*)*vern*, *isnel irnel*, *peior pigor*, proclitic *per pir*, *premier* (*i*), *semblar* (*i*), *serven* (*i*), *serventes* (*i*), *sevals* (*i*), *trebalhar* (*i*), *tremblar* (*i*). In *disnar*, *ivern*, *isnel* only i is found. In some dialects there is an alternation of e and i, e being used when there is an í in the next syllable, i when there is none: *fenit*, *sirvén*. In *vezi*<*vīcīnum* the e probably goes back to V. L.: cf. Fr.

4. In a few dialects e in hiatus with a following vowel becomes i: *crear criar*, *leal lial*, *prear priar*, *preon prion*, *real rial*.

5. In many dialects of the north and west e has a tendency to become a before r: *guerentia garensa*, *merce marce*, *pergamen pargamen*.

6. In some dialects there is a tendency to assimilate e to an á in the next syllable: *delgat dalgat*, *gigant iaian*, *deman* (*a*), *semblar* (*a*), *serrar* (*a*), *tremblar* (*a*). So *de vás* (§ 42, 1)>*da vás*>*dávas*; hence *daus*, under the influence of *deus*>*de ves*.

INTERTONIC SYLLABLE.

45. The term *intertonic* is applied to the syllable that follows the secondary (§ 18) and precedes the primary accent. In this position all vowels, except a, regularly disappeared in popular words, probably between the 5th and the 8th century[1]; a apparently remained: **bŭllĭcāre*>boiar (bollegar),

[1] The period of the fall of the intertonic vowel covers, in part, the period of the voicing of intervocalic surds (§ 65); sometimes the vowel fell too soon for the surd

bŏnĭtātem > bontat, **carrĭcāre* > carcar cargar, *caballĭcāre* > cavalcar cavalgar, *cĕrĕbĕllum* > cervẹl, *cīvĭtātem* > ciutat, *cŏllŏcāre* > colcar colgar, *dēlĭcātum* > delcat delgat, *excommūnĭcāre* **excommĭnĭcāre* > escomeniar, *vĕrēcŭndia* > vergọnha; *calamĕllum* > calamẹl, *invadĕre* **invadīre* > envazir, *margarīta* > margarida, *mīrabĭlia* > miravilha, *parav(e)rēdus* > palafrẹs.

1. The vowel is preserved in a number of words in which it originally bore the secondary accent (§ 18): *abbrèviáre* > *abreuiar*, *cupìditátem* > *cobeitat*, **erìciónem* > *erisso*; on the other hand, **cominìtiáre* (through **comìn'tiáre*) > *comensar*, *partìtiónem* (through **pàrtiónem*) > *parso*. Cf. *Zs.*, XXVII, 576, 684, 693, 698, 701, 704. When kept, the vowel is sometimes altered: **carōnea* **caròneáta* > *caraunhada*, **cupìditósus* > *cobeitos cobitos*, *papìliónem* > *pabalho*.

2. The prefix *mĭnus*– was reduced to *mis*– (or *mes*–) in Gaul, perhaps at the close of the Vulgar Latin period: **mìnus-prĕtiat* > *mespreza*. Cf. P. Marchot, *Phon.*, pp. 43, 44.

3. *Mostier* is from **monistĕrium*, altered, by the influence of *ministĕrium*, from *monastērium*. *Comprar* is from V. L. *comperare*. *Calmelh calmelha* (cf. *calamel* above) are Provençal formations from *calm*. *Caresma* or *caresme*, from *quadragēsĭma*, is probably French. *Anedier* < *anatarium* shows the influence of *anèt ánet* < *anătem* (§ 50).

4. In learned words the vowel is generally preserved: *irregulár*, *irritár*, *pelicán*, *philozophía*. The vowel is, however, often altered, the exchange of e and i being particularly frequent: *esperít*, *femeníl*, *orifán*, *peligrí* (*e*), *soteirán* (*sotrán*) < *subterraneum* influenced by *dereirán* and *primeirán*.

46. Very often the intertonic vowel was preserved by the analogy of some cognate word or form in which that vowel was stressed: dev*i*nár through *devín*, fin*i*mén through *finír*, guerr*e*iár through *guerréia*, noir*i*dúra through *noirír*, obl*i*dár through *oblít*, pert*u*sár through *pertúsa*, re*u*sar through *reúsa*, serv*i*dór through *servíre*.

---

to be voiced, sometimes it did not. The relation of the fall of unstressed vowels to the development of intervocalic consonants, in French, has been examined by L. Clédat in the *Revue de philologie française*, in a series of articles beginning XVII, 122. Cf. P. Marchot, *Phon.*, pp. 84–90.

1. In such cases the preserved vowel is sometimes altered, the exchange of e and i being especially common: _avinén, covinén, sovinénsa_, cf. _venír, ven_; _enginhár, enginhós_, cf. _genh_; _envelzír_, cf. _vil_; _gememén_, cf. _gemír_; _issarnít_ (_eissernít_), from _excĕrnĕre_; _randóla_, from _hirŭndŭla_, perhaps influenced by _randón_; _temerós_ (_o_), from _*timorōsus_, influenced by _temér_; _traazó_ (_i_), from _traditiōnem_, with a substitution of suffix; _volentiérs_, from _voluntarius_, under the influence of _volén_ < _volentem_.

PENULT.

47. (1) The vowel of the penult of proparoxytones fell in many words in Vulgar Latin, especially between a labial and another consonant, and between two consonants one of which was a liquid: _*avĭca_ > _*auca, cŏm(i)tem, cŏmp(u)tum, dēb(i)tum, dŏm(i)nus_[1]; _alt(e)ra, vĭg(i)lat, cal(i)dus, vĭr(i)dem_; _frig(i)dus, nĭtĭdus_ > _*nĭttus, pŏs(i)tus, pūtĭdus_ > _*pūttus_.

(2) The classic Latin _-culus_ comprises an original _-clus_ (_sæclum_) and an original _-culus_ (_aurĭcŭla_). In popular Latin both were _-clus_ (_*macla, ŏclus_, etc.), to which was assimilated _-tŭlus_ in current words (_vĕtŭlus_ > _vĕclus_, etc.).

(3) Many popular words which in Vulgar Latin had very generally lost the vowel were for some reason introduced into southern Gaul in their classical forms, and not a few were adopted both in the uncontracted and in the syncopated state: _fragĭlem_ > frágel (cf. Fr. _fraile_, It. _frale_), _jŭvĕnem_ > iọve (cf. Fr. _iuevne_); _clĕrĭcum_ > clẹrgue _clĕr'cum_ > clẹrc, _dēbĭtum_ > dẹute _dēb'tum_ > dẹpte, _flēbĭlem_ > frẹvol _flēb'lem_ > frẹble, _mal'habĭtum_ > malaute _mal'hab'tum_ > malapte, _nĭtĭdum_ > nẹde _*nĭttum_ > nẹt, _hŏmĭnem_ > ome _hŏm'nem_ > omne, _pŏpŭlum_ > pọbol _pŏp'lum_ > pọble.

1. _Cŏgnĭtum_ seems to have become _*cónhede_, whence _coinde cuende conge_. Cf. § 79, Gnd, Gnt.

---

[1] _Domnus_ may be the older form.

48. The unaccented penult vowels that had not already fallen dissappeared, in most cases, in the transition from Latin to Provençal: **carrĭcat*> carca, *cŏllŏcat*> cǫlca, *cŭrrĕre* > cǫrre, *spathŭla*> espatla, **ĕssĕre* (= *ĕsse*)> ẹstre, *ī(n)sŭla* isla, *pĕssĭmum* > pẹsme, *pōnĕre* > pǫnre, **rīdĕre*> rire, *tabŭla*> taula, *tŏllĕre*> tǫlre.

1. A apparently was more tenacious than other vowels, and frequently remained as an indistinct e: *anătem* > ánet, which, being associated with the diminutive ending *-ét*, became anét (cf. modern Pr. *anèdo*); *cannăbim* > cánebe (learned?); *cŏlăphum* > *cólebe > cǫlbe, but *cŏl'phum* > cǫlp; *Stĕphănum* > Estẹve; *lampăda* > lámpeza; *ŏrgănum* > órguene (later orguéne) órgue; *ŏrphănum* > ǫrfe; *raphănum* > ráfe; *Rhŏdănum* > Rǫzer; **sēcăle* (= *sĕcāle*) > séguel (but cf. modern *segle selho*). Cf. A. Thomas in the *Journal des savants*, June, 1901, p. 370. See also P. Marchot, *Phon.*, pp. 90–94. Cf. § 45, footnote. It is noteworthy that *cólebe ultimately lost its penult, while the other words lost the final syllable or none.

49. Under certain conditions, however, a vowel which had not fallen in the Latin of southern Gaul was often kept in Provençal. It was then probably indistinct in sound, and was written usually *e*, but occasionally *o*.

(1) After c′, g′, or y the vowel was apparently retained in some dialects and lost in others. When the c′, g′, or y was intervocalic, forms with and without the vowel are about equally common; when the c′, g′, or y was preceded by a consonant, forms with the vowel predominate, and after cons. + c′ the vowel was apparently never lost. After intervocalic c′: *cŏcĕre* (= *cŏquĕre*)> cǫire cǫzer, *dīcĕre*> dire dízer, *dūcĕre* > düire *düzer (condücir dedüzir), *facĕre*> faire *fázer (fazedǫr, etc.), *gracĭlem* > graile, **nŏcĕre* (= *nŏcēre*) > nǫire nǫzer, *placĭtum*> plach, *sŏcĕrum*> sǫzer (sǫgre is from *sŏcrum*), **vŏcĭtum* (= *vacuum*)> vuech. After intervocalic g′ or y: *bajŭlus*> bailes, *fragĭlem*> frágel, *imagĭnem*> imáge, *lĕgĕre* > lẹire legír (through *lẹger?), *rĭgĭdum*> rẹide rẹge, *rĭgĭda*>

ręgeza, **tragĕre* (= *trahĕre*) > traire tragír (through *tráger?). After cons. + c′: *carcer* > cárcer, *crēscĕre* > cręisser, *nascĕre* > náisser, *pascĕre* > páisser, *parcĕre* > párcer, **tŏrcĕre* (= *tŏrquēre*) > tǫrzer. After cons. + g′ or y: *angĕlum* > ángel (learned?), **cŏll'gĕre* (= *cŏllĭgĕre*, through *cŏllĭgo* etc.) > cǫlre cuelher colhír, **dē-ēr'gĕre* (= *ērĭgĕre*) > dęrdre dęrzer, **fŭlgĕrem* (from *fŭlger* = *fŭlgur*) > fọuzer, *jŭngĕre* > iọnher, *margĭnem* > marge, *plangĕre* > planher, *vĭrgĭnem* > vęrgena vęrge.

(2) After ks, s, ss, and sy the vowel was apparently retained in some dialects and lost in others: *dīxĕrunt* > diron dissęron (through *dísseron)[1], *dūxĕrunt* > düystrent düissęron (*dúisseron), *fraxĭnum* > fraisne fraisse, *traxĕrunt* > traissęron (*tráisseron), *tŏxĭcum* > tuęissec; *asĭnum* > asne ase, *mĭsĕrum* > miser (learned), **prē(n)sĕrunt* > pręson prezęron (*prezeron), *rema(n)sĕrunt* > remastrent remasęron (*remáseron); **ĕssĕre* (= *ĕsse*) > ęstre ęsser (used in Rouergue, Limousin, Marche, and Dauphiné), **mĭssĕrunt* (= *mīsĕrunt*) > męstrunt (męsdren) mesęron (*męsseron), *passĕrem* > pásser; **cō(n)siĕre* (= *consuĕre*) > cǫser (cozír is from V. L. **cosīre*).

(3) Between a labial and a dental the vowel was apparently kept: *cŭpĭdum* > cǫbe, *fēmĭna* > fęmena fęme (but *fēm'na* > fęmna), *jŭvĕnem* > iọve, **lūmĭnem* > lüme (*lūmen* > lüm), *hŏmĭnem* > ómen óme (but *hŏm'nĕm* > omne), *tĕpĭdum* > tębe, *tĕrmĭnum* > tęrme. Cf. § 48, 1.

(4) Between a dental and a guttural the vowel remained long enough for the guttural to become y (§ 52; § 65, G): *mĕdĭcum* > *mędegu > *mędeye > mędže (= *mege*). If the first consonant was a liquid or a nasal, the vowel apparently allowed the guttural to become y in some dialects, but not in

---

[1] The change of accent, in this verb and others, was due to the analogy of the first and fourth conjugations (cantęron, sentíron) and to the influence of the second person plural (dissętz).

others: **carrĭcat* > caria carga, *clĕrĭcum* > clẹrie clẹrgue, *mŏnăchum* > monie mongue. *Caballĭcat* > cavalga, *cŏllŏcat* > cọlca cọlga show an earlier fall. In *clĕr'cum* > clẹrc the fall goes back to Latin times.

50. Some learned proparoxytones kept for a while both post-tonic vowels (usually written *e*), but most of them ultimately either shifted their accent to the penult (§ 17, 1) or dropped their final syllable: *domĕstĭcum* > domẹstegue, *lacrĭma* > lágrema, *mĕrĭtum* > mẹrite, *hŏrrĭda* > ọreza, *rēgĭmen* > régeme; *fĭstŭla* > feštóla, *fragĭlem* > fragíl, *mĕrĭtum* > merít, *tĕrmĭnum* > termíni; *diacŏnum* > diágue, *flēbĭlem* > frẹvol (cf. *flēb'lem* > frẹble), *nĭtĭdum* > nẹde (cf. **nĭttum* > nẹt), *ōrdĭnem* > órde, *pŏpŭlum* > pọbol (cf. *pŏp'lum* > pọble), *prīncĭpem* > príncep prínce. Cf. § 47, (3).

FINAL SYLLABLE.

51. As early as the 8th century, in popular words, the vowels of final syllables fell, the fall occuring first, perhaps, after liquids: *hĕrī* > ẹr, *malĕ* > mal; *bŏnŭs* > bos, *cŏlăphŭm* > cọlp, *cōgĭto* > cüg, *panĕm* > pan, *prĕtiŭm* > prẹtz.

(1) Latin a, however, remained, being generally pronounced ạ: *audiăm* > auiạ, *bŏnă* > bonạ, *fīliās* > filhạs.[1]

(2) Latin final ī probably remained in all dialects later than the 8th century, and in some until the beginning of the literary period: *hábuī* > águi > aguí. Before it fell, it changed an accented ẹ in the preceding syllable to ị: see § 27.

(3) Latin i and u remained if they were immediately

[1] In most of the modern dialects (but not in Gascony and lower Languedoc) this a has become o: *rosa* > *roso*. But in the Limousin dialects and some others -as > -a: *rosas* > *rosa*.

preceded by an accented vowel: *fuī* > füi, *mĕī* > mẹi, *sŭī* > sọi; *cavum* **caum* > chau, *dĕus* > dẹus, *ĕgo* **ĕo* **ĕu* > ẹu, *rīvum rīum* < riu. In such cases the two vowels formed a diphthong.

(4) Before final nt Latin e, u remained as e, o: *cantent* > canten, *vēndunt* > vẹndon.

1. In Aude, Tarn, Aveyron, Corrèze, and a part of Haute-Garonne, final ī was preserved as late as the 12th century: *pagadi*, *salvi*, *soli*. See *Rom.*, XIV, 291–2. Such forms occur also in Vaud and Dauphiné. Cf. *Gram.*, II, p. 82.

2. In the extreme east there are traces of final *-ōs*: *aquestos*, *ellos*, *tantos*.

3. *Grau* for *gra* < *gradum*, *niu* for *ni* < *nīdum* are Catalan. *Amiu* for *amic* < *amīcum*, *chastiu* for *chastic* < *castīgo* belong to the dialect of Forez, and point to a very early fall of the guttural in that dialect. Cf. § 65, D, G.

4. *Ferre* beside the commoner *fer* < *fĕrrum* is perhaps due to the analogy of *terra*. *Aire*, *vaire*, beside *air* < *aĕrem*, *vair* < *varium*, probably show the influence of the numerous nouns in *-aire* (*amaire*, etc.); cf. § 52, (1). *Fores* is doubtless a cross between *foras* < *fŏras* and *fors* < *fŏris*. *Nemes* beside *nems* < *nĭmis*, *senes* beside *sens* < *sĭne* perhaps follow the analogy of *fors fores*. For *colbe*, see § 48, 1. *Reide rede* perhaps owes its -e to *rege*: § 49, (1).

5. *Coma*, beside *com*, *con*, *co* < *quōmŏ(do)*, apparently owes its -a to the analogy of the adverbs *bona* and *mala* and other adverbs of manner. For a different explanation, see J. Vising in the *Tobler Festschrift* (*Abhandlungen Herrn Prof. Dr. Tobler .... dargebracht*, 1895), p. 113.

6. *Demanes* < *de manu ĭpsa* lost its -a perhaps under the influence of *ades*.

7. E seems to have been preserved in the second person singular of some verbs, to distinguish it from the third person: co(g)nōscis < conọisses, *co(g)nōscit* > conọis.

52. When the fall of the vowel would have resulted in an undesirable consonant group at the end of a word, the vowel was retained as an indistinct e: *dŭbĭto* > dọpte, *lŭcrum* > lọgre.

The principal groups that call for a supporting vowel are:

(1) a consonant and a liquid; (2) a labial and a dental; (3) in proparoxytones, a consonant and a c′ or c originally separated by the vowel of the penult; (4) in proparoxytones, a consonant and an m or n originally separated by the vowel of the penult. Ex.: *ĭnter*>ẹntre; *aptum*>apte; **dōdĕcim*> dọtze, *jūdĭco*>iütge; *Jacŏmus>Iacmes, *asĭnum*>asne.

If the word was a paroxytone, and the first consonant was a palatal and the second an r, the supporting vowel stood between the two: *major*>maier, *mĕlior*>mẹlher, *mŭlier*> mọlher, *pĕjor*>pẹier, *sĕnior*>sẹnher. Otherwise the supporting vowel followed the consonant group.

The four classes of groups (aside from the palatal + r just mentioned) will now be examined in detail:—

(1) Examples: *alter*>autre, *Carŏlus*>Carles, *dŭplus*> dọbles, **ĕssĕre*>ẹstre, *fabrum*>fabre, **mĕr(ŭ)lum*>mẹrle, *nŏster*>nọstre, *pauper*>paubre, *pŏp(ŭ)lum*>pọble, *pōnĕre*> pọnre, *recĭpĕre*>recẹbre, *rŭmpĕre*>rọmpre, *tŏllĕre*>tọlre, *vŏlvĕre*>vọlvre; *mascŭlum*>mascle, etc.; *flēb(ĭ)lem*>frẹble, etc. Under this head is included r–r (*cŭrrere*>cọrre, *quærĕre*>quẹrre), but not ll and rr (*bĕllum*>bẹl, *fĕrrum*>fẹr). In Provençal the first element was often changed, later than the 8th century, into a vowel, original b and v becoming u, and d, t, c, g, and y being turned to i: *bĭbĕre*>bẹure, *scrībĕre*>escriure, **mŏvĕre*>mọure, *plŏvĕre*>plọure, *vīvĕre*> viure; *latro*>laire, *matrem*>maire, *radĕre*>raire, **rīdĕre*> rire, *vĭtrum*>vẹire; *desīdĕro*>desire, etc.; *amător*>amaire, *servītor*>servire, etc.; *dīcĕre*>dire, *dūcĕre*>düire, *facĕre*> faire, *gracĭlem*>graile, **tacĕre*>taire; *frīgĕre*>frire, *weigăro* gaire, *lĕgĕre*>lẹire; *bajŭlum*>baile. Apparent exceptions to the rule are intervocalic cl, gl, which were probably reduced to single consonants before the 8th century: *ŏc(ŭ)lum*>ọlh, *vĭg(ĭ)lo*>vẹlh.

1. The rare forms *frair*, *pair*, beside regular *fraire*, *paire*, are perhaps due to the alternative forms *air aire*, *vair vaire* (§ 51, 4). There may be a similar explanation for *faur* = *faure* < *faber*, and for the learned *albir* = *albire* < *arbĭtrium*. *Sor*, beside *sorre* < *sŏror*, probably developed first as a proclitic.

(2) Examples: *cŭbĭtum* > cọde; *cŏmĭtem* > comte; *dēbĭtum* > dẹpte dẹute, § 47, (3); *dŏmnum* > domne; *dŭbĭto* > dọpte; *hŏspĭtem* > ọste; *sabbătum* > sapte.

1. *Azaut* seems to be post-verbal from *azautar* < *adaptāre*. *Escrit* < *scrīptum* probably shows the influence of *dit* < *dīctum*. *Malaut*, beside *malaute malapte* < *mal'habĭtum*, is perhaps reconstructed from the feminine *malauta* on the model of *aut*, *auta*. *Set* < *sĕptem* must have developed as a proclitic.

(3) Examples: *jūdicem* > iütge[1]; *pŏllĭcem* > pọuze; *quīndĕcim* > quinze; *salĭcem* > sauze; *sĕdĕcim* > sẹdze;—*canŏnĭcum* > canonge canọrgue,[2] § 49, (4); *clĕrĭcum* > clẹrge clẹrgue (§ 48, 2); *mĕdĭcum* > mẹtge; *mŏnăchum* > monge mongue mọrgue,[2] § 49, (4); *vĭndĭco* > vẹnie; *viatĭcum* > viatge, etc.

1. The forms *poutz*, *sautz*, beside *pouze*, *sauze*, would seem to indicate that lc' did not require a supporting vowel in all dialects.

2. **Ficotum* (= *jĕcur*), a fusion of συκωτόν ('fig-fattened') and *fīcus*, combined with **hĕpăte* (= *hĕpar*), became *fẹ́catu *fẹcitu *fẹgidu, and then, through the influence of the familiar ending -igu (= *ĭcum*), *fẹdigu > fẹtge. See G. Paris in *Miscellanea linguistica in onore di G. Ascoli*, 1901, p. 41; H. Schuchardt in *Zs.*, XXV, 615, and XXVIII, 435; L. Clédat in *Revue de philologie française et de littérature*, XV, 235. *Pege*, for *peich* < *pĕctus*, seems to be due to the analogy of *fetge*.

(4) Examples: *æstĭmo* > esme; *dĕcĭmum* > dẹsme; *fraxĭnum* > fraisne; *incūdĭnem* > enclütge (cf. § 80, Dn); **metĭpsĭmum* > medẹsme; *pĕssĭmum* > pẹsme; *prŏxĭmus* > prọsmes.

1. Faim < *facĭmu(s)* doubtless lost its -e through the analogy of the alternative form fazẹm < **facĭmu(s)* and of the usual endings -ám, -ẹm.

---

[1] The *tg* in this word is probably due to the influence of *iutiar* < *jūdĭcāre*.

[2] The forms with *r* may be due to dissimilation or to the influence of *clergue*.

(5) In some dialects, at least, by, mby, mny, py, rny required a supporting vowel: *rŭbeum* > rọtge, *cambio* > camie, *sŏmnium* > songe suenh, *apium* > ache api, *Arvĕrnium* > Alvẹrnhe; ratge (= *rabiem*) is probably French. Original lm, rm, sm required a supporting vowel in some dialects but not in others: *hĕlm* > ẹlme ẹlm, *ŭlmum* > ọlme ọlm, *palmum* > palm; **ĕrmum* (ἔρημον) > erm, *fĭrmum* > fẹrm, *gĕrmen* > gẹrme; *spasmum* > espasme.

(6) Many verbs regularly have an -e in the first person singular of the present indicative: desire, dọpte, iütge, etc. By the analogy of these, -e often appears in the first person singular of verbs which need no supporting vowel: *remīro* > remir remire. By the analogy of the preterit (águi, füi, etc.), -i is very often substituted for this -e: azọr azọri, cant canti, prẹtz prẹzi, etc.

53. Many late words preserve the final vowel as *-e*: benigne, bisbe < *epĭscŏpum*, digne (cf. denhar), mixte (cf. mẹst), regne (cf. reing), signe (cf. sẹnh). Cf. § 50; (for cọlbe) § 48, 1; and (for cọinde, etc.) § 47, 1. Learned formations from nouns in *-ium* usually end in *-i*, simply dropping the *-um*: capitọli, edifici, empẹri, iüzízi, martíri (martíre), negọci, offíci, periüri, remẹzi, servízi, vici. Similar forms in *-i* were sometimes taken from the accusative of nouns and adjectives in *-ius*: Boẹci < *Boëthium*, prọpri (prọpre) < *prŏprium*, savi < *sabium*.

1. It should be remembered that the Latin words, at the time of their adoption, had undergone various phonetic changes in the clerical pronunciation: cf. § 15. A form *remezi*, for instance, presupposes a pronunciation of *remĕdium* as remẹðiu(m).

3. CONSONANTS.

54. The Latin consonants which we have to consider are: b, c (= k), d, f, g, h, j (= y), l, m, n, p, qu (= kw), r, s, t, v (= w), x (= ks). To these we must add the Vulgar Latin w coming from u̯, and y coming from e̯, i̯: see § 40, (2). Furthermore, in words borrowed from Germanic dialects we find b, ð, h, k, þ, w, which call for special notice; and, in words borrowed from Greek, ch, k, ph, th, z.

The Latin d, f, j, l, p, t call for no remark at present. Latin h, in popular speech, became silent very early (*hŏc* > *ŏc*, *hŏmo* > *ŏmo*), and, although an attempt was made to restore it in polite speech, it left no trace in the Romance languages: cf. *Rom.*, XI, 399. Double consonants were pronounced distinctly longer than single ones: *annus*, *ĭlle*, *ŏssum*, *tĕrra*.

55. Latin b, c, g, m, n, qu, r, s, v, w, x, y show the following developments in popular Latin speech:—

B between vowels became, through failure to close the lips tightly, β (bilabial v), from the 1st to the 3d century of our era: *habēre* > aβẹre. The same change took place, to a certain extent, when the b was not intervocalic, but we have few, if any, traces of it in Provençal. Between vowels, even in learned words, the clerical pronunciation was probably β or v until the 7th century. Cf. V.

C before a front vowel (e, i), as early as the 3d century, doubtless had, in nearly all the Empire, a front or palatal articulation; that is, it was formed as close as possible to the following vowel[1]: *cĕntum* > c′ĕntu, *dūcĕre* > dūc′ĕre. The next step was the introduction of an audible glide, a brief y, between the c′ and the vowel[2]: c′yẹntu, dục′yere. By the

[1] Compare, in English, the *c* of *coo* and the *k* of *key*.

[2] Compare the old-fashioned pronunciation of words like *card*, *kind*.

5th century this c′y had developed into a kind of ty, the c′ having been drawn still further forward: t′yẹntu dụt′yere. Through a modification of the y-glide, the group then became, in the 6th or 7th century, tš or ts: tšẹntu tsẹntu. See H. Schuchardt, *Voc.*, I, 151, and *Ltblt.*, XIV, 360; P. E. Guarnerio, in *Supplementi all' Archivio glottologico italiano*, IV (1897), pp. 21–51 (cf. *Rom.*, XXX, 617); G. Paris, in the *Journal des savants*, 1900, 359, in the *Annuaire de l'École pratique des Hautes-Études*, 1893, 7, in the *Comptes rendus des séances de l'Académie des Inscriptions*, 1893, 81, and in *Rom.*, XXXIII, 322; W. Meyer-Lübke, *Einf.*, pp. 123–126; F. G. Mohl, *Zs.*, XXVI, 595; P. Marchot, *Phon.*, pp. 51–53; P. Meyer, *Die Aussprache des* c *und* t *im klassischen Latein*, 1902. Cf. G and X.[1]

G between vowels, before the accent, disappeared in some words in at least a part of the Empire: *le(g)ālis*, *li(g)āmen*, *re(g)ālis*, (*realis* is attested for the 8th century); *ĕgo*, generally used as a proclitic, everywhere lost its g; on the other hand, g was kept in *castigāre*, *fatigāre*, *ligāre*, *negāre*, *pagānus*. G before a front vowel (e, i), by the 1st or 2d century, was pronounced g′ (cf. C): *gĕntem* > g′ĕnte, *fragĭlis* > frag′ilis. As early as the 4th century this g′, through failure to form a close articulation, opened into y[2]: yẹnte, fráyilis. Before an accented e or i an intervocalic y disappeared, in the greater part of the Empire, being fused with the vowel: *magĭster* > mayịster > maẹster, **pagēnsis* > payẹsis > paẹsis, *regīna* > reyịna > reịna.[1]

M and n, when final, were weak and indistinct from the earliest times, except in monosyllables; by the 3d or 4th cen-

---

[1] For final *-ci*, *-gi* in plurals, see § 92, (2).

[2] Before this, *frīgĭdus* had become frịgdus in Italy and Gaul.

tury they had probably disappeared altogether from the end of polysyllables: damnu, nọme; but jam, non.

N before spirants (f, j, s, v), except in the prefixes *con–* and *in–*, became silent during the Republican period, the preceding vowel, if it was short, being lengthened by compensation[1]: *mē(n)sis*, *pē(n)sare*. If the syllable *con–* or *in–* was not recognized as a prefix, the n fell: *co(n)sul*, *co(n)ventum*, *i(n)fas*. In learned and newly constructed words the *n* was pronounced. Cf. M.

Qu, gu before o or u were reduced to c, g in the 1st or 2d century: see W.

R before s, in a number of words, became s in the Republican period: *deōrsum* > deōssum, *dŏrsum* > dŏssum, *sūrsum* > sūssum; so, in a part of the Empire, *pĕrsĭca* > pĕssĭca, *vĕrsus* (preposition) > vĕssus. Early in our era ss after a long vowel was reduced to s: deōsu, sūsu.

S was probably always voiceless, or surd, in classic Latin, but became voiced between vowels, in Gaul, at the end of the Vulgar Latin period: *casa*. To initial s + consonant an i or e was prefixed, at first, no doubt, after a word ending in a consonant: *in schŏla* > in iscŏla; this process began in the 2d century and had become general by the 4th.

V, originally pronounced w, became β probably in the 1st century: *vīvĕre* > βīβĕre. Before u, *v* regularly disappeared, but it was restored by analogy in many words: *flavus* > flaus, *ŏvum* > ŏum, *rīvus* > rīus; but also *ŏvum*, *rīvus*, by the analogy of *ova*, *rivi*. In the greater part of the Empire v apparently fell also before an accented o: *pavōnem* > paōne, *pavōrem* > paōre. Cf. W. When a β, representing either b or v,

[1] It is natural to suppose that the n, in falling, nasalized the vowel; but no trace of this nasality remains.

became contiguous to a following consonant, it changed to u: *_avĭca_ > aβĭca > auca, _gabăta_ > gaβata > gauta, *_flavĭtat_ > flaβĭtat > flautat. In several words rv became rb in Latin: _vervēcem_ > berbēce berbīce, _cŏrvus_ > cŏrbus, _cŭrvus_ > cŭrbus.

W coming, in the 2d or 3d century, from u̯ (§ 40) differed from Latin _v_, then pronounced _β_, but was probably identical with Germanic _w_: _dēbuī_ > dẹbwi̯, _placuī_ > placwi̯ _sapuit_ > sapwit, _tĕnuis_ > tẹnwis. W fell between a consonant and o or u: _antīquus_ > antịcus, _battuo_ > batto, _carduus_ > cardus, _cŏquus_ > cọcus, _distĭnguo_ > distịngo, _mŏrtuus_ > mọrtus; so _eccu'hŏc_ > Pr. acọ. Cf. Qu.

X (=ks) was reduced to s, in the 2d or 3d century, before a consonant or at the end of a word of more than one syllable: _sĕstus_, _sĕnes_; but _sĕx_. So the prefix _ex_– > es– before any consonant but s: *_exgaudēre_ > Pr. esiauzir, *_exlucēre_ < Pr. esluzir, *_exmĭttĕre_ > Pr. esmẹtre. Ex– + s apparently became either ex– or ess–: *_exsanguinātum_ > Pr. eissancnat, *_exserāre_ > Pr. eissarrar esserrar, *_exsaritāre_ > Pr. eissartar, *_exsĕquĕre_ > Pr. essẹgre, *_exsŭrgĕre_ > Pr. essọrger, *_exsūcāre_ > Pr. eissügar essügar.

Y coming, in the 2d or 3d century, from e̯ or i̯, (§ 40) coincided with Latin _j_: _habeam_ > abya, _eāmus_ > yamus, _tĕneat_ > tẹnyat; _audio_ > audyo, _fīlia_ > fịlya, _vĕniat_ > vẹnyat. As early as the 4th century the groups dy, gy were reduced to y; and ly, ny probably became l', n': _mĕdius_ > mẹdyus > mẹyus, _corrĭgia_ > corrịgya > corrẹya; _mĕlior_ > mẹlyor > mẹl'or, _tĕneo_ > tẹnyo > tẹn'o.

56. Germanic b, ð, h, k, þ, w call for special mention:—

B did not participate in the change of Latin intervocalic b to _β_: _roubôn_ > Pr. raubar. The words containing it were evidently adopted after this phonetic law had ceased to operate.

ð, þ were pronounced by the Latins as d, t: **waiðanjan*> *wadanyāre> Pr. gazanhar (It. guadagnare), *þrëscan*> *trescāre> Pr. trescar.

H, at the beginning of a word, was lost in the greater part of the Empire, including southern Gaul: *hapja*> *apya> Pr. apcha. H between vowels was lost in some words and replaced by kk in others: *spëhôn*> Pr. espiar, *fëhu*> Pr. fẹu, *jëhan*> *yekkīre> Pr. gequir. Ht was regularly replaced by tt: *slahta*> *sclatta> Pr. esclata; but *wahta*, perhaps borrowed later, became Pr. gaita.

K, in southern Gaul, did not take the palatal pronunciation before front vowels: *skërnon*> Pr. esquernir, *skina*> Pr. esquina, *skiuhan*> Pr. esquivar, **rîk-ĭtia*> Pr. riquẹza; only the derivatives of *Franko* (doubtless Latinized early) show palatalization, as **Francia* > Pr. Fransa. G, however, seems to have been palatalized: *gîga*> Pr. giga, *geisla*> Pr. giscle. Before a, in words introduced early, k and g were treated like Latin c and g: *kausjan*> Pr. cauzir chauzir, *gâhi*> Pr. gai iai; see § 11, (1).

W was vigorously pronounced, and, through reinforcement of its velar element, came to be sounded gw: *warjan*> *warīre gwarīre> Pr. garir, *wërra*> *wẹrra gwẹrra> Pr. guẹrra.

57. Greek ζ, θ, κ, φ, χ did not exactly correspond to any Latin consonants: —

Z, whatever may have been its original pronunciation, received in Vulgar Latin the value dy, which then, like any other dy, became y: **zelōsus* (from ζῆλος) = dyelọsus yelọsus > Pr. gelọs. The infinitive ending *-ίζειν*, introduced in such words as *βαπτίζειν*> *baptizāre* = bapti(d)yāre, became very common in the form -ịdyāre -ịyāre, and was used to make new verbs: *wërra* + *ἵζειν* > * werr ịdyāre gwerr ịyāre > Pr. guerrẹiar.

θ, in the popular speech of Rome, was replaced by t: similarly χ was replaced by c: *σπαθή* > *spatha* = spata; *χορδή* > *chŏrda* = cọrda.

κ was apparently intermediate in sound between Latin c and g; it was generally replaced by the former, but sometimes by the latter: *κατά* > *cata*, *κυβερνᾶν* > *gubernare*.

φ, in Greek, was in early times (perhaps until the 4th century of our era) a strongly explosive p; it then developed into f. In words borrowed by the Romans in the early period it was replaced by p; in later words it was sounded f: *κόλαφος* > *cŏlăphus* = cọlapus, *φασίολος* > *phaseŏlus faseŏlus*.

58. The fate of all these consonants in Provençal depended largely on their position in the word: we must therefore distinguish *initial*, *medial*, and *final* consonants. In a general way, the first tended to remain unchanged, the second to weaken, the third to disappear. Furthermore we must separate single consonants from consonant groups: the latter resisted change better than the former; but a group consisting of dissimilar elements tended to assimilate them.

INITIAL CONSONANTS.

59. A consonant preceded by a prefix was treated as an initial consonant as long as the character of this preceding syllable was recognized: *de-cadĕre* > decazẹr, *de-pĭngĕre* > depẹnher, *præ-parāre* > preparar, *re-cordāre* > recordar, *re-patriāre* > repairar, *re-pausāre* > repausar, *se-dūcĕre* > sedüire. If, however, the initial syllable ceased to be recognized as a prefix, the following consonant was treated as a medial con-

sonant: *præpŏsĭtum* > prebọst, *retŏrta* > redọrta; so, perhaps, *profŭndum* > preọn. The rare rebọnre (beside repọnre) < *re-pōnĕre* has the special sense 'to bury'.

SINGLE INITIAL CONSONANTS.

60. B, d, l, m, n, p, r, s, t underwent no change: ben, dọn, lọc, mẹ, nau, pauc, rius, si, tü.

1. For *cremetar* < **tremitāre*, see Meyer-Lübke, *Einf.*, § 194. For *granolha* < **ranŭcŭla*, see Körting, *ranuculus*.

61. C, c′, f, g, g′, β, y suffered some change. C, g must be distinguished from c′, g′: § 55, C, G.

C, g before o, u remained unchanged: *colōrem* > colọr, *cūra* > cüra; *gŭla* > gọla, *gŭtta* > gọta. Before a they changed only in the north and northeast, where they became (perhaps from the 7th to the 9th century) respectively tš and dž: *campus* > camps champs; *gaudēre* > gauzir iauzir.

C′ > ts, which just before and during the literary period was reduced to s: cælum > cẹl sẹl, *cīvitātem* > ciutat ciptat siptat. Eor g′, see Y.

Y, comprising Latin dy, g′, gy, j, and z, became dž (except in Béarn, where it remained y): *diurnālem* > iornal (yornal), *deō(r)sum* > iọs; *gĕlus* > gẹls, *gentīlem* > gentil (yentil), *gȳrāre* > girar; *jam* > ia, *jŏcum* > iọc (yọc), *jŭvĕnem* > iọve; *zelōsus* > gelọs.

F remained unchanged, except in Béarn and a part of Gascony, where it became h: *famem* > fam ham, *fĭdem* > fẹ hẹ, *fŏcum* > fọc hüc, *fŏlia* > fuelha huelha.

β > v (the dentilabial spirant), except in Béarn, Gascony, and parts of Languedoc, where it became b: *vĕnit* > ven be, *vĕntum* > vent bent, *vĕrsus* (§ 55, R) > vẹs bẹs, *vōs* > vọs bọs.

1. In a few words β, owing to Germanic influence, was replaced by w > gw: *vadum* + *watan* > *gua*, *vastare* + *wŏst* > *guastar*. So *vagīna* > *guaina*, *Vascŏnia* > *Gasconha*. Cf. gw below.

INITIAL GROUPS.

62. There are three classes of groups: those ending in l or r, those ending in w, and those beginning with s: —

(1) Bl, br, cl, cr, dr, gl, gr, pl, pr, tr underwent no change: *blasphemāre* > blasmar, *brĕvem* > brẹu, *clarus* > clars, *crŭcem* > crọtz, *drappus* > draps, *glaciem* > glatz, *gradum* > gra, *plēnum* > plẹn, *precāre* > pregar, *trans* > tras. Gras is from *grassus*, a fusion of *crassus* and *grossus*. For grọcs < *κρόκος* see § 57, *κ*.

(2) Gw (Germanic w) and kw (Latin qu) were reduced, perhaps in the 10th century, to g and k, except in the west, where the w was retained: *wahta* > gaita guaita, *warjan* > garir guarir, *wĕrra* > gẹrra guẹrra, *wīsa* > gisa guisa; *quando* > can quan, *quare* > car quar. It should be noted that the *u* was commonly kept in the spelling (especially before e and i) after it had ceased to be pronounced, *gu* and *qu* being regarded merely as symbols for "hard" g and c. For cinc < *quīnque*, see § 87, kw. Sw remained in *suavem* > suau.

(3) To groups beginning with s a vowel had been prefixed in Vulgar Latin (§ 55, S); this vowel appears in Provençal as e. Sc′ apparently did not occur in any popular word; sl early became scl; the other groups (sc, scl, scr, sp, st, str) remained unchanged, except that in the north and northeast sc > stš before a: *scala* > escala eschala, *schŏla* > escọla, *slahta* > * *sclatta* > esclata, *scrībĕre* > escriure, *spīna* > espina, *stare* > estar, *strĭngĕre* > estrẹnher.

MEDIAL CONSONANTS.

63. (1) It is well to note at the outset that when, through the fall of an unaccented vowel (§ 51), an early Provençal b, d, dz, dž, g, z, or ž was made final or contiguous to a final s, it became voiceless: *ŏpus* > ọbus > ọbs ọps, *ŏrbum* > ọrbu > ọrb ọrp: *datum* > dadu > dad dat, *vĭrĭdem vĭrdem* > vẹrde > vẹrd vẹrt; *prĕtium* > prẹdzu > prẹdz prẹts (written *pretz*), *vōcem* > vọdze > vọdz vọts (written *votz*); *mĕdium* > mẹyu mẹdžu > mẹdž mẹtš (written *meg* or *mech*); *amīcus* > amigus > amigs amics, *largum* > largu > larg larc; *rīsum* > rizu > riz ris; *basium* > bažu > baiž baiš (bais). The combination tžs, however, loses either its second or its third element: **gaudios* > gautšs > gautš or gauts (both of them often written *gaugz*); so *nŏctes* > nuetšs > nuetš or nuets (*nuegz*). For *apud* > *ab ap am an*, see § 65, P, 2.

(2) Under the same conditions, y became i: *vĭdeo* > vẹyo > vẹy vẹi, *pĕjus* > pẹyus > pẹys piẹis.

(3) Under the same conditions, ð, coming from intervocalic d, fell when final, but became t before s: *audit* > auði > auð au; *crūdus* > cruðus > cruds crüts. So *crūdum* > crü, *fĭdem* > fẹ, *fraudem* > frau, *gradum* > gra, *nīdum* > ni, *nōdum* > nọ, *pĕdem* > pẹ, *sapidum* > sabe, *tĕpidum* > tẹbe; *grados* > grats, *nōdus* > nọts, *nūdus* > nüts, *pĕdes* > pẹts. The two sets of forms influenced each other: hence *degras*, *fes*,[1] *nis*, *pes*, etc.; *crut*, *grat*, *not*, *nut*,[1] etc.

(4) Under the same conditions, β, coming from v or from intervocalic b, became u if preceded by a vowel, but fell if preceded by a consonant: *bĭbit* > bẹβi > bẹβ bẹu, *vīvit* > βịβi > βịβ vịu, *claves* > claβes > claβs claus, *vīvus* > βīβus >

---

[1] *Fes*, *nut*, which quite supplanted the regular forms, perhaps show the influence of *res*, *mut*.

βịβs vịus; *salvet* > sal, *salvum* > sal, *sĕrvit* > sẹr, *nĕrvos* > nẹrs, *salvus* > sals, *sĕrvus* > sẹrs. Sometimes, however, final β preceded by a consonant, instead of falling, became f: *salvet* > salf, *salvum* > salf, *sĕrvit* > sẹrf, *vŏlvit* > vọlf; it may be that these are the only regular forms for cons. + β *when final*, and that *sal*, *sier* are due to the analogy of *sals*, *siers*.

(5) Under the same conditions, final n, if preceded by a vowel, was kept in the extreme west, parts of the north, and all the southeast and east, but fell everywhere else; n before s was generally kept only in the southeast and east: *bĕne* > be ben, *canem* > ca can, *sŏnum* > so son[1]; *bŏnus* > bos bons, *mansiōnes* > maisọs maisọns. If the n was preceded by a consonant (r), the fall seems to have been even commoner: *cŏrnu* > cọr cọrn, *tŏrno* > tọr tọrn; *diŭrnus* > iọrs iọrns. Provençal n coming from nn never falls: *annus* > ans.

(6) Under the same conditions, g, representing original c or g, became c after o or u, and after other vowels either became c or was changed to i (which fused with a preceding i): *fŏcum* > fọc, *lŏcus* > lọcs, *paucum* > pauc, *Hŭgo* > Uc; *Aureliăcum* > Aurẹlhac, *dīco* > dic di, *Henrīcum* > Enric Enri, **trago* > trac trai. The forms with c are the commoner; they have been most persistent in the west.

(7) The vocalization of l before s (*malus* > maus) is a different phenomenon from the foregoing, and will be treated by itself: § 65, L.

(8) An m or an n that becomes contiguous to final s often develops into mp or nt, but oftener (judging from the spellings) does not: *nĭmis* > *nems nemps*, *rēmos* > *remps*; *annos* > *ans anz*, *gĕnus* > *ges gens genz*.

---

[1] By analogy of such double forms, n is sometimes added to a few words ending in a vowel: *fŭit* > *fo fon*, *prō* > *pro pron*.

(9) Between a liquid or a nasal and a final s, a b or a p generally fell, unless supported by the analogy of a form in which the b or p was final: *ambos* > *ams ambs*, *cŏrpus* > *cors*, *tĕmpus* > *tems temps*; cf. *balbs* (*balb*), *orbs* (*orb*).

1. The d, n, t of the proclitics *ad*, *quid*, *in*, *aut*, *et* will be treated under Final Consonants.

64. Final ts from any source, in Provence, Limousin, and a part of Languedoc and Gascony, was reduced, during the literary period, to s: *amātis* > amatz amas, *habētis* > avẹtz avẹs, *dīcit* > ditz dis, *grandes* > granz grans, *latus* > latz las, *prĕtium* > prẹtz prẹs. On the other hand, in a part of Limousin (especially in Limoges), and also in Dauphiné, -ts, in the second person plural of verbs, became t: habētis > avẹt.

SINGLE MEDIAL CONSONANTS.

65. The single medial consonants will now be considered separately, in alphabetical order: —

β, coming from b or v, became v; except in the west and a part of the centre, where, if it remained intervocalic, it changed to b: *habētis* > avẹtz abẹtz, *debēre* > devẹr debẹr, *faba* > fava faba; *avārum* > avar, *æstīva* > estiva, *brĕvem* > brẹu,[1] *clavem* > clau, *dīe Jŏvis* > diiọus, *lĕvat* > lẹva, *novĕlla* > novẹla nabẹra (Gascon), *vīvus* > vius. When the preceding or following vowel was o or u, a *β* before the accent fell in most dialects, being fused with the vowel: *abŭndare* > aondar abondar, *gŭbĕrnare* > goernar governar, proclitic *ŭbĭ* > ọ, *prŏbare* > proar, *sŭbĭnde* > soẹn sovẹn sobẹn, *trĭbūtum* > treüt; *Lŭdovīcus* > Lozoics, *Provĭncia* > Proẹnsa Provẹnsa, *novĕllum* > noẹl novẹl, *novĕmbrem* > noembre novembre, *pavōnem* > paọn, *pavōrem* > paọr (cf. § 55, V).

[1] Cf. § 63, (4).

1. The perfect endings *-avi* etc., *-ivi* etc. had lost their v in Latin. For avia, etc., see § 87, *β*.

2. *Abans*, beside *avanz*, *avan* < *ab ante*, apparently shows the influence of Pr. *ab* = *apud*. *Abet* < *abiĕtem* (§ 40, 1) is unexplained: cf. Italian *abete*. *Abora* is a Provençal compound of *ab* and *ora*. *Trap*, beside *trau* < *trabem*, is doubtless from the nominative *traps* < *trabs*, which seems to have been differentiated in meaning from the V. L. nominative *trabis*.

3. *Brey*, *grey*, *ney*, beside *breu* < *brĕvem*, *greu* < **grĕvem*, *neu* < *nĭvem* (cf. § 25, 1, *e*), have been subjected to the attraction of *grey* < *grĕgem*, *ley* < *lēgem*. *Greug* is a post-verbal noun from *greuiar* < **grĕviare*.

4. *Massis* < *massīvus*, *natiz* = *natius* < *natīvus* seem to have been influenced by *mestis* < *mixtīcius*.

5. *Paziment* = *pavamen* owes its z perhaps to the analogy of *aizimen*.

6. In purely learned words, *b* and *v* were written as in Latin: *diabol*, *diluvi*.

C, from the 4th to the 6th century, was voiced to g, and then developed like any other g. See G.

1. After au, apparently, c did not change: **auca* (< **avĭca* < *avis*) > *auca*, *pauca* > *pauca*, *rauca* > *rauca*, * *traucare*(? < * *trabucare*) > traucar. Cf. § 65, P, 3.

2. In purely learned words, c remained unchanged: *vocal*. *Alucar aluchar*, *aluc* seem to be learned formations patterned after *anteluсānus* and Low Latin *lucānus*.

C′, when it became contiguous to a consonant, through the fall of the unaccented vowel of the penult, was reduced to i: * *cŏcĕre* > cọire, *dīcĕre* > diire dire, *dīcĭtis* > ditz, *facĕre* > faire, *facĭmu(s)* > faim, *facĭtis* > faitz, *fēcĕram* > fẹira, *fēcĕrunt* > fẹiron, *gracĭlem* > graile. When it remained intervocalic, it was assibilated during the transition period (§ 55, C); in most of the Provençal territory it became dz, which during the literary period was simplified to z; but in some dialects of the south and the northwest it resulted in idz (later iz), an i-glide having developed before the consonant while it was still palatal: *aucĕllum* > auzẹl, *jacēre* > iazẹr, *lĭcēre* > lezẹr, *lūcēre*>lüzẹr lüzir lüisir, *placēre*>plazẹr plaizẹr; *crŭcem*> crọz crọiz crọis (see §§ 63, 64), *dīcere*>dízer, *dīcit*>ditz dis, *dūcit*>dütz düs, *facit*>fatz fas, *jacet*>iatz ias iays, *pacem*> patz pas pais, *placet*>platz plas plais, *verācem*>verais, *vōcem* >vọtz vọiz.

1. *Aucel*, beside *auzel*, perhaps belongs to a dialect in which c′ was not voiced after au: cf. C, 1. See § 80, Bc′.

2. *Iasser*, beside *iazer*, seems to be due to *ias*<*jacet* and *iassa*<*jaceat*.

3. For *desma deima*, see S, 1.

4. In purely learned words, c′>ts: *acĭdum*>aci.

D, in a part of the west, remained unchanged; elsewhere, during the Vulgar Latin period, it opened into ð, which fell in the 11th century and earlier in parts of the north and east, and in the rest of the Provençal territory became z as early as the first part of the 12th century: *audīre*>auzir auir audir,[1] *audit*>au,[2] *cadit*>ca, *crudēlem*>cruzẹl cruẹl crudẹl, *fīdat*>fia, **gaudo*>gau, *hŏrrĭda*>ọreza, *hŏrrĭdum*>ọre, *laudo*>lau, *alauda*>lauzẹta laudẹta, *rīdat*>ria, *tradĕre*> trazir trair tradir, *vidēre*>vezẹr vẹr vedẹr, *vĭdet*>vẹ. When ð became contiguous to a following consonant (except final s), it changed to i: *cupĭditātem*>cobeitat, *divīdĕre*>divire,[3] *traditōrem*>traidọr.[4]

1. *Crey*, beside *cre*<*crēdo*, follows *dei*<*dēbeo*, *vei*<*vĭdeo*. *Mercey*, beside *merce*<*mercēdem*, shows the influence of *grey*<*grĕgem*, *lei*< *lēgem*, and perhaps French *fei*<*fĭdem*. Cf. β, (3).

2. *Grau*=*gra*<*gradum*, *niu*=*ni*<*nīdum* belong to the Catalan dialect, in which ð fell before the 8th century: *gradum*>*graðu*>*gra-u* >*grau*, the u being preserved through combining into a diphthong with the a.

---

[1] Also *auvir*, probably a local development of *auir* or *auzir*; and *aurir*, doubtless from *auzir* in a dialect that confuses r and z. See R, 2 and S, 2.

[2] Cf. § 63, (3).

[3] The i from ð fuses with the preceding i.

[4] *Trachor* has been influenced by *trach*, past participle of *traire*.

3. In purely learned words, d remained: *odi*<*ŏdium*.

F is very rare (cf. § 59). The few examples appear to show that f (presumably in the 6th century or earlier) became β, and then developed like any other β (see β): *Stĕphănum* > Estẹve, *co(n)fortāre?* > * coβortar > * coortar > conortar (through the common use of the double forms, *con–*, *co–*), *gryphum* > griu, *raphănum* > rave rafe, * *refusāre* > rehusar refusar, **prefŭndum* (=*pro–*) > preọn. Nevertheless, cof in *cŏphĭnum*, defọrs < *de fŏris*, grifọ, profiẹg < *profĕctum*, rafe, would seem to indicate that in some words, possibly less popular at the outset, f was retained.

1. In purely learned words, f was kept: *antifona*, *Caifas*, *philozophia*.

G, representing original c and g, had a varied development.[1] For the fall of g in some words in Vulgar Latin, see § 55, G.

(1) Before a, g remained in the greater part of the territory, but in the north and east it early became y; and this y was generally retained in the eastern dialects (often fusing with a preceding i), while in most of the northern it developed into dž (cf. Y): *amīca* > amiga amiia amia, *dīcam* > diga dia, *mīca* > miga miia mia,[2] *pacāre* > pagar paiar, *precāre* > pregar preiar; *castigāre* > castigar castiar, *legālem* > leial leyal lial, *ligāmen* > liam, *lĭgātum* > legat liat, *plaga* > plaga plaia, *regālem* > reial, *rūga* > rüa.

(2) Before o and u (ü), g was preserved, except in a few words which (doubtless in Vulgar Latin times) lost it either in all or in many dialects: *acūtum* > agüt, *secŭndum* > segọn, *secūrus* > segürs; * *a(u)gūrium* > agür aür, *a(u)gŭstum* >

---

[1] Intervocalic c and g have been studied by H. Sabersky, *Zur provenzalischen Lautlehre*, 1888, pp. 8-19.

[2] *Mica micha* are from **mīcca* = *mīca* + *cĭccum*.

agọst[1] ahọst, proclitic *ĕgo* > ęu, **fagŏttum* > fagǫt, *figūra* > figüra, *Hugōnem* > Ugọ. For a g that becomes final or contiguous to final s, see § 63, (6): *amīcus* > amics amis, *Auriăcum* > Auriac, *cŏcum* (= *cŏquum*) > cǫc, *jŏcus* > iǫcs, *Ludovīcum* > Lozoic Lozoi, *prĕco* > pręc; *castīgo* > chastic chasti.

(3) Between the last two vowels of a proparoxytone, g, early in the Provençal period, became y, which developed into dž before the literary epoch; cf. § 49, (4): *clĕrĭcum* > clęrge, **coratĭcum* > coratge, *domĭnĭcum* > dimẹnge, *manĭca* > mania, *mĕdĭcum* > męge, *mŏnăchum* > monge, **paratĭcum* > paratge, *viatĭcum* > viatie. In some dialects, however, the vowel of the penult, after liquids and nasals, fell too early for the g to become y: clęrgue,[2] dimęrgue, mongue.

1. *Amiu*, *chastiu* belong to the dialect of Forez; so perhaps *fau* < *fagum*, *preu* < *prĕco*. These forms indicate a very early fall of the g in the dialect to which they belong. Cf. § 51, 3.

2. In purely learned words, Latin g remains unchanged: *paganōrum* > *paganor*.

G′ became y during the Vulgar Latin period (§ 55, G). See Y.

1. In purely learned words the letter *g* was retained, but it was doubtless pronounced dž: *astrologia*.

L remained: *colōrem* > colọr, *male* > mal, **volēre* (= *velle*) > volẹr. Before final s, l became u in most dialects, in some as early as the 10th century: *malos* > maus, *talis* > taus; *l* was written, however, long after l had been vocalized. Under the influence of forms in which -ls > -us, final l became u in the southwest and in some other regions: *Aprīlem* > abriu. Cf. § 74, (2).

---

[1] For the reduction of *au* to *a* see § 41.

[2] *Clerc* is from **clĕrcum*, which must have existed contemporaneously with *clĕrĭcum*.

1. For Gascon l > r, see § 10.

2. *Orifan*, beside *olifan* < *elephantem*, is probably French.

L′ will be considered, as ly, under Groups, § 73, Ly.

M remained: *amāre* > amar, *hŏmo* > om, *timōrem* > temọr.

1. Occasionally final *-am* rhymes with *-an* (*afan* : *fam*, *portam* : *avan*); this would seem to indicate an indistinct pronunciation of the final nasal in some dialects. Cf. *aven* = *avem* < *habēmu(s)* in the *Nobla Leyczon*. Cf. § 167, 2.

N remained: *bŏnas* > bonas, *donāre* > donar, *lūna* > lüna. For n final or contiguous to final s, see § 63, (5): *fīnis* > fis fins, *panem* > pa pan.

1. In *canorgue*, *dimergue*, *morgue*, beside *canonge*, *dimenge*, *monge*, the r may be explained by the analogy of *clergue*.

2. *Menhs meins*, beside regular *mens* < *mĭnus*, show the influence of the alternative forms *genhs geins* and *gens* from *ingĕnium* (see § 73, Ny).

3. *Iassey* (= *iasse*, the latter part of which may be from *exin* = *exĭnde*), *tey* (= *te* < *tĕnet*), used by Marcabru, are doubtless due either to a mistaken imitation of conventional borderland forms (see § 25, 3) or to the analogy of *crei* = *cre* < *crēdo* (*crei* itself being due to the analogy of *dei* < *dēbeo*, *vei* < *vĭdeo*).

N′ will be considered, as ny, under Groups, § 73, Ny.

P, from the 4th to the 6th century, was voiced to b: *capĭllum* > cabẹl, *rīpa* > riba, **sapēre* (= *sapĕre*) > sabẹr, *trepalium* > trebalh; *capit* > cap (§ 63), *sapis* > saps.

1. In some borderland dialects p > v, as in French: *saver*. *Evescat*, *evesque*, beside *bisbat*, *bisbe*, are French.

2. *Apud*, used as a proclitic, became for some reason in Vulgar Latin **apu*, which developed regularly into **abu* and, after the fall of intertonic vowels, *ab*. This *ab* assimilated its b more or less to a following consonant, becoming *ap* before voiceless consonants, *am* before nasals; *am*, used before dentals, became *an*: hence we have four forms, *ab*, *ap*, *am*, *an*. *Amb* seems to be a fusion of *am* and *ab*; when used before a consonant with which mb did not readily combine, it expanded into *ambe*. See Elise Richter, *Zs.*, XXVI, 532.

3. In some dialects, apparently, p was not voiced after au: *sapuĕrunt* **sapwĕrunt* **saupĕrunt* > *saubron saupron*. Cf. § 65, C, 1.

4. In purely learned words, p remains: *epifania*.

R remained: *amāra* > amara, *durāre* > dürar, *ĕrat* > ẹra. Final rs was reduced to s, in most dialects, during and after the literary period: *priōres* > priọrs priọs (*Girart*); the reduction apparently began in Limousin as early as the 12th century (Bertran de Born rhymes iọs and flọrs).

1. Final r began to fall in many dialects in the 14th century. At present it has disappeared all through the south and west: *amōrem* > *amou*, *flōrem* > *flou*.

2. In some dialects (especially those of Gard and Hérault) intervocalic r and z were confused, probably during the literary period: *gyrāre* > *girar gisar*; conversely *audīre* > *auzir aurir*. Cf. *Revue des langues romanes*, XL, 49, 121.

S was voiced to z, probably from the 4th to the 6th century: *pausa* > pausa, *presĕntem* > presen; *rīsum* > ris (§ 63).

1. An s that became contiguous to n was changed, in a few dialects, to r: *almosna almorna*, *disnar dirnar*. In modern Limousin and some of the dialects of Dauphiné, Languedoc, and Gascony, s has disappeared before nasals: *asne ane*, *caresma carema*, *disnar dinar* (so *blasmar blamar*, *desma dema*); the fall began during the literary period. S before a consonant in many of the modern dialects, and final s in some, has become i: *asne aine*, *caresma careima* (so perhaps *desma deima*, *pruesme prueime*); some traces of this change occur in texts of the literary period. Cf. *Zs.*, XXIII, 413. *Isla*, in Limousin, became *ilha* (perhaps through *iyla*): cf. *Zs.*, XXIII, 414. Cf. § 78.

2. In some southeastern dialects intervocalic z after au has changed to v: *causa cauva* (so *auzir auvir*); possibly the *auvent* of the *Boeci*, v. 23, is to be connected with this.

T, from the 4th to the 6th century, was voiced to d: *amāta* > amada, *natālis* > nadals, *servitōrem* > servidọr; *habētis* > avẹtz avẹs avẹt (§§ 63, 64), *latus* > latz las, *natum* > nat. For a t which became contiguous to r (*amātor* > amaire), see § 52, (1), and § 70, Tr.

1. In some dialects of the south and southeast, final t fell shortly after the literary period: *amātum* > *amat ama.*

2. *Tōtus*, in Gaul, became *tōttus* as early as the 4th century: hence Pr. *tota totas*. For *meteis* < *met-ĭpse* see § 131, (2).

3. *Espaza* (beside *espada*) < *spatha*, was perhaps influenced in its pronunciation by the spelling of the Latin word. *Ez*, coming from *et* before a vowel, shows the influence of *az* (< *ad* + vowel) and *quez* (< *quĭd* + vowel). *Grazal*, 'grail', is perhaps a cross between **cratella* < *crater* and *gradale*, 'service-book'; so *grazalet*. *Grazir grazire* (cf. *agradar*) is perhaps altered from an earlier **grazar* < **gratiare*. *Mezeis* < *met-ĭpse*, *mezesmes*, *meesmes* (beside *medesmes*) < **met-ĭpsĭmus* have been subjected to the analogy of *ez* < *et* and *quez* < *quĭd* or of *ĭd ĭpsum*: § 131, (2).

4. *Appoestat* must be French.

5. *Calabre* < **catabŏlum* seems to have been assimilated to *Calabria*.

6. In purely learned words, t remains: *eternal*.

W will be considered, as gw, under Groups, § 72, *β*w.

X is a symbol for ks: see Groups, § 79, Ks.

Y, representing Latin dy, g', gy, j, and z (cf. § 55, G, Y; § 57, Z) had a varied development.

(1) When it became contiguous to a following consonant (§§ 45, 49), it changed to i: *adjutāre* > *ayudāre* > ay'dar > aidar, *medietātem* > meitat; *cōgitāre* > cüidar, *frīgĕre* > frire, *lĕgĕre* > lẹyre, *propagĭnem* > probaina, *rĭgĭda* > rẹida, * *tragĕre* > traire; *bajŭlus* > bailes.

(2) When it remained intervocalic, it became dž in most of the territory, but in the northeast and parts of the north it was not changed: *audiam* > auia, *in-ŏdiare* > enoiar, *invĭdia* > envẹia, *invĭdiōsus* > enveiọs enveyọs, **gladia* > glaya, *mediānum* > meian, **pŏdiāre* > poiar, *radiāre* > raiar, *sordĭdior* > sordẹier, *vĭdeat* > vẹia; *fragĭlem* > fragel; **exagiāre* > assatiar essaiar essayar, *corrĭgia* > corrẹia corrẹya, *fagea* > faia faya, *regiōnem* > reiọ; *dīe Jŏvis* > diiọus, *major* > maier, *pĕjor* > pịẹier, *pejōrem* > peiọr, *trŏja* > trọia; *baptizāre* > bateiar. For

a dž or a y that became final or contiguous to final s, see § 63, (1), (2): *audio*>auch, *in ŏdio*>enuẹg (plural enuẹtz enuẹg) enọi, *gaudium*>gauch, *gladium*>glai, *mĕdium*>mẹg mẹi, *hŏdie*>ọi, *pŏdium*>puẹg pọi, *radium*>rai; *fŭgit*>füg füi, *grĕgem*>grẹy, *lēgem*>lẹg (pl. lẹitz) lẹi, *lĕgit*>liẹg, *magis* mais,[1] *rēgem*>rẹi, _*tragit_>trai; *exagium*>essai; *pĕjus*> piẹis.

(3) Before accented e or i, y disappeared (doubtless in Vulgar Latin: § 55, G), except in some western dialects, where it became dž: *vagīna*>guaïna, _*legīre_ (=*lĕgĕre*)> legir,[2] *magĭster*>maẹstre maiẹstre magẹstre, _*pagē(n)sis_> paẹs pagẹs, *regīna*>reïna, *sagĭtta*>saẹta saiẹta sagẹta.

1. *Detz ditz* < *dĭgĭtus* are irregular and unexplained. The word is irregular in some other Romance languages, notably in Italian. Cf. Gröber's *Grundriss*, I, p. 507.

2. *Glavi*, beside *glai* (and learned *glazi*) < *gladium*, is supposed by some to show the influence of Celtic *cládibo*. Cf. Körting; also H. Schuchardt, *Zs.*, XXV, 345.

3. *Messér* seems to be a contraction (due to proclitic use) of _*messeyer_ = *mes*, 'my', + _*seyer?_ < _*sĕyor_ = *sĕnior* (cf. A. Lindström, *L'analogie dans la déclinaison des substantifs latins en Gaule*, 1897–8, pp. 292–3).

4. In purely learned words, *di*, *g*, *gi*, *z* are retained, the *g* being pronounced presumably as dž, the *z* as z: *odi*, *fragil*, *regio*, *canonizar*.

MEDIAL GROUPS.

66. Medial groups may be conveniently classified as follows: — A. *Double Consonants* (1); B. *Groups of Dissimilar Consonants:* groups ending in l (2), groups ending in r (3), groups ending in w (4), groups ending in y (5), groups beginning with l, m, n, r, or s and not ending in l, r, w, or y

[1] *Magis* was probably reduced to *mais* in Vulgar Latin.

[2] *Legir* may have been reconstructed on the basis of *leg* < *lĕgit*.

(6), all other groups (7). They will be treated in the order indicated.[1]

1. It should be noted that the prefixes *ad-*, *sub-* regularly assimilate their d or b to the following consonant: **ad-rīpāre* > *arribar*, *sub-venīre* > *sovenir*. *Sosrire*, *sosterrar*, *sostraire* show a substitution of prefix, due, no doubt, to the analogy of *sospirar*, *sostener*.

1. DOUBLE CONSONANTS.

67. In general, the double consonants became single, in the 9th or 10th century (perhaps earlier before the accent), but underwent no other change save those described in §§ 63, 64: *abbātem* > abat, *sĭccum* > sẹc, *rĕddo* > rẹt, *affībulāre* > afiblar, *aggregāre* > agregar, *flamma* > flama, *pĭnna* > pẹna, *cappa* > capa, *passum* > pas,[2] *mŭttum* > mọt, *advenīre* **avvenīre* > avenir.

(1) Cc before a, in the east and northeast, became tš; elsewhere, c; *bŭcca* > bọca bọcha, *vacca* > vaca vacha.

(2) Ll, in some southern dialects, became l′; elsewhere, l: *capĭllum* > cabẹl cabẹlh, *grȳllum* > gril grilh, *mantĕllum* > mantęl mantęlh, *villānus* > vilas vilhas. It is possible, however, that -llī regularly became l′ in Limousin, while ll before other vowels was not palatalized: *caballum* > caval, *caballī* > cavalh; *illī* > ilh, *illōs* > ẹls; this would account in part for the frequent occurrence of *lh* in the poems. For final ls and l, see § 65, L: *illos* > ẹls ẹus, *vallem* > val vau. For Gascon l > r, see § 10: *appĕllat* > apęla apęra.

(3) Rr, when intervocalic, seems generally to have been distinguished from r during the literary period and later: *cŭr-*

[1] For the groups ending in y, cf. L. J. Juroszek, *Ein Beitrag zur Geschichte der jotazierten Konsonanten in Frankreich*, in *Zs.*, XXVII, 550 ff. The groups ending in y and those containing c or g have been studied by H. Sabersky, *Zur provenzalischen Lautlehre*, 1888.

[2] S is generally written *ss* between vowels, to distinguish it from *s* = z.

rĕre > cọrre, **corrŭptiāre* > corrossar, *errāre* > errar, *tĕrra* > tẹrra. Occasionally, however, rr is found in rhyme with r.

2. Groups Ending in L.

68. The groups of two consonants will be treated in alphabetical order. It will be seen that bl, rl, sl remained unchanged; ml developed a glide consonant between its two members; pl, tl, βl, and yl respectively voiced, assimilated, and vocalized their first element; while cl, gl were fused into l'. For an explanation of this last phenomenon, see § 79.

Bl > bl: *nĕbŭla* > nẹbla, **oblītāre* > oblidar, *sabulōnem* > sablọn.[1]

βl > ul: *fabŭla* **faβla* > faula, *sibilāre* **siβlāre* > siular, *tabŭla* **taβla* > taula.

Cl > l': *genŭcŭlum* > genọlh, *ŏcŭlum* > ọlh, *sĭtŭla* **sĭcla*[2] > sẹlha, *vĕtŭla vĕcla*[2] > vẹlha. In learned words we find gl, cl: **e(c)clĕsia* > glẹiza, *joculārem* > ioglar, *sæcŭlum* > sẹgle sẹcle.

C'l > il: *gracĭlem* > graile.

Dl > dl, which during the literary period became ll and then l: *mŏdŭlum* > *mọdle mọlle.

Gl > l': *vĭg(ĭ)lat* > vẹlha. Tẹula < *tēgŭla* is irregular: cf. *Archivio glottologico italiano*, XIII, 439, 459.

Ml > mbl: *sĭmĭlāre* > semblar, *trĕmŭlat* > trembla. In *sembrar* we find an r < l due perhaps to the analogy of membrar < *memorāre.*

Pl > bl: *cōpŭla* > cọbla, *dŭplum* > dọble. Learned words have pl: *duplicar.*

Rl > rl: *Carŏlus* > Carles, *hōrolŏgium* > orlọi, **paraulare* > parlar.

---

[1] Most of the words in this category are semi-learned: cf. *fabla* and *faula*. See § 55, B.

[2] See § 47, (2).

Sl > sl: *ī(n)sŭla* > isla. For *ilha*, see § 65, S, 1.

Tl > tl, which during the literary period became ll and then l: *rŏtŭlum* > rọtle rọlle, *spathŭla* > espatla espalla espala. In really popular words tl had become cl in Vulgar Latin.[1]

Yl > il: *bajŭlus* > bailes. Cf. § 65, Y, (1).

69. A group of three consonants remained unchanged, except that double consonants became single: *ambulāre* > amblar, *implēre* > emplir, *avŭncŭlus* > avọncles, *cĭrcŭlus* > cẹrcles, *mascŭlus* > mascles, **afflammāre* > aflamar, *inflāre* > enflar, *ŭngŭla* > ọngla, *emplastrum* > emplastre.

1. *Selcle*, beside *cercle*, seems to show an assimilation of the r to the l of the next syllable. *Empastre*, beside *emplastre*, has been influenced by *pasta*. *Emblar* is probably from V. L. **imbolare* = *involare*.

3. GROUPS ENDING IN R.

70. The groups of two consonants will be treated in alphabetical order. It will be seen that br, gr, lr, nr generally remained unchanged; mr, sr, zr (and sometimes lr, nr) developed a glide consonant; cr, pr voiced, and βr, c'r, dr, tr, yr vocalized their first element.

Br > br: *fabrum* > fabre, *fĕbrem* > fẹbre, *līb(ĕ)rum* > libre.

βr > ur: *bĭbĕre* > bẹure, débēr' hábẹo > deβ'r–áyo > deurái, *faber* > faure;[2] **mŏvĕre* (= *mŏvēre*) > mọure, *plŏvĕre* > plọure.

Cr > gr: *acrem* > agre, *lacrĭma* > lagrema, *lŭcrum* > lọgre, *macrum* > magre, *sacrāre* > sagrar, *sŏcrum* > sọgre.[3] In late learned words we find cr: *secret*.

C'r > ir: *cŏcĕre* > cọire, *dīcĕre* > dire, *dūcere* > düire, *facĕre* > faire. Cf. § 49, (1).

Dr > ðr > ir: *divīdĕre* > devire, *quadrum* > caire, vídēr' há-

[1] See § 47, (2).
[2] We find also *faur*: cf. § 52, (1), 1.
[3] *Sozer* is from *sŏcĕrum*: cf. § 49, (1).

bệo > veđ'r–áyo > veirái. After au, apparently, đ simply disappeared: *clauděre* > claure. Late learned words have dr: *quadrupedi.*

Gr, in popular words, was reduced to r in Vulgar Latin in parts of the Empire: *fra(g)rāre* > *frarar *flarar flazar, *intě(g)rum* > entẹr entiẹr, *nĭ(g)rum* > nẹr niẹr,[1] *pere(g)rīnum* > peleri, *pĭ(g)rĭtia* > perẹza; these forms occur in Gascony, Rouergue, and Limousin, but forms with gr are found in the same region. Elsewhere, in these same words, and everywhere, in more bookish words, gr remained in Vulgar Latin; this gr was kept in most of the Provençal territory, but was changed to ir in Dauphiné, Auvergne, and Languedoc: **de-grădum* > degra, *fragrāre* > flairar, *integrāre* > enteirar, *intěg-rum* > entẹgre entẹir,[2] *nĭgrēscěre* > negrezir, *nĭgrum* > nẹgre nẹir,[2] *peregrīnum* > pelegri, *pĭgrĭtia* > pigrẹza. Purely learned words have gr everywhere: *agricultura.*

G'r: see Yr.

Lr usually remained unaltered, but in some dialects became ldr[3]: válēr' hábệo > valrai valdrai, *vólēr' hábệo > volrai voldrai.

Mr > mbr: *camĕra* > cambra, *memorāre* > membrar, *nŭmě-rum* > nọmbre.

Nr usually remained unaltered, but in some dialects became ndr[3]: *cĭněrem* > cẹnre cẹndre, *dīe Věněris* > divenres divendres, *in-gěnerāre* > engenrar, *Henrīcum* > Enric, *expōněre* > espọnre espọndre, **gěněrem* (= *gěnus*) > genre, *gěněrum* > genre gendre,

---

[1] For the vowel of nẹr niẹr, see § 25, 1, (*e*).

[2] *Enteir, neir* seem to have lost final e under the influence of numerous adjectives in *-er -ier -ieir* < *-arium.*

[3] In the modern dialects the d is probably commoner than it was in the old literary language; it occurs in Bordeaux, Languedoc, and Provence.

honorāre > onrar ondrar, *prĕndĕre* > penre, *tenēr' habeo* > tenrai tendrai, *venīr' habeo* > venrai vendrai.

Pr > br: *capra* > cabra, *cŭperāre* > cobrar, *erĭpĕre* > erẹbre, *ŏpĕra* > ọbra, *pauper* > paubre, **pĭperāta* > pebrada, *recĭpĕre* > recẹbre, *sŭperāre* > sobrar, *sŭper* > sọbre. Purely learned words have pr: *caprin*. It is uncertain whether *paupre* (beside the usual *paubre*) is a Latinism or represents some dialect in which au prevented voicing.

Sr > str: **ĕssĕre* (= *ĕsse*) > ẹstre. For ẹsser, see § 49, (2).

Tr > dr > ðr > ir: *amātor* > amaire, *fratrem* > fraire, *latro* > laire, *mater* > maire, *ŭtĕrem* > ọire, *pĕtra* > pẹira, *Pĕtrus* > Pẹires, *petrōnem* > peirọ, *petrōsus* > peirọs, *pre(s)bȳtĕrum* (*Einf.*, § 140) > prevẹire, *servītor* > servire, *vĭtrum* > vẹire. Learned words have dr and tr: **poenĭtĕre* > *penedre* (*penedir*), *impetrāre* > *impetrar*.

Yr > ir: *frīgĕre* > frire, *lĕgĕre* > lẹyre.

Zr > zdr: *mīsĕrunt* + **mĭssĕrunt* > *mẹzron mẹsdron.

1. *Redebre* (beside *rezemér*) < *redīmere* has apparently been influenced by *recebre*. The Burgundian *sor* for *sobre* comes from the prefix *sŭr-* (*sŭr-rīdēre*, etc.). *Perri* < **pētrīnum* is probably French.

71. A group of three consonants nearly always remained unchanged, except that double consonants became single: *ŭmbra* > ọmbra, *arbŏrem* > arbre, *sepŭlcrum* > sepulcre, **canc(e)rōsus* > cancrọs, **addīrēctum* > adrẹit, *fŭndĕre* > fọndre, *ardĕre* > ardre, **offerīre* > offrir, **Hungaría* > Ongria, *rŭmpĕre* > rọmpre, *apprĕssum* > aprẹs, *asprum* > aspre, *ŭltra* > ọltra, *intrāre* > entrar, *mo(n)strāre* > mostrar, *mĭttĕre* > mẹtre. Lβr and rg'r, however, regularly became ldr and rdr, and llr became ldr to the same extent as lr (q. v.): *absŏlvĕre* > absọldre (*absolvre* is probably a Latinism), *pŭlvĕrem* > pọldre; **dē-ēr' gĕre* > dẹrdre; *tollĕre* > tọlre tọldre. Rmr became rbr

in *marmor*>marbre (also marme). Prendre often became penre (perhaps to distinguish it from pendre<*pĕndĕre*) through the analogy of genre gendre, etc.; the first r having been lost by dissimilation.

1. The four-consonant group sbtr is reduced to str in *prestre*<*prĕsbўter*. *Prever* is perhaps a proclitic syncopation of a V. L. **preβiter*. Cf. § 78, 1.

4. GROUPS ENDING IN W.

72. This class includes not only Latin gu̯, qu̯, but all combinations of consonant + u̯, cf. § 40, (2). A w thus evolved seems to have developed like Germanic w (cf. § 56, W): it became gw (assimilating the preceding consonant, unless that consonant was a liquid or a nasal), and then was reduced, before the literary period, to g, cf. § 62, (2). Pw, however, had a quite different history, owing, on the one hand, to the affinity of its two labial elements, and, on the other, to the stability of the voiceless stop, which prevented the assimilation that we find in βw>ww.

1. G. Körting (*Zs*., XXII, 258) would explain through the analogy of the perfects in *-cui* all other perfect forms which in Provençal have g and c corresponding to Latin *-ui* etc.

βw>ww>gw>g: *habuĭssem*>agues, *dēbuit*>dec (§ 63); **co*(*g*)*nōvuit* (cf. Meyer-Lübke, *Gram*., II, p. 357)>conoc, **crevuĭstī*>creguist, **movuĭsset*>mogues, **plŏvuit*>ploc. We seem to have the same combination in Germanic *treuwa*> tregua trega (*treva* is probably French).

1. The diphthong of *aic*=*habuī* is probably not a phonetic development. The first and third persons of the preterit, *aic* and *ac* (<*habuit*), have been differentiated after the pattern of the present—*ai* and *a*.

Dw>gw>g: **sĕduit*>sec.

1. *Vezoa*<*vĭdua* must be an early learned word: *veuva* is doubtless French.

Kw > gw > g: *antīqua* > antiga, *ĕqua* > ęga, *æquālem* > egal (*engal* has received through a mistake in etymology the prefix *en–* or *e–* < *in–*), *nŏcuit* > nǫc, *placuĭstī* > plaguist, **sĕquĕre* (= *sĕqui*) > sęgre, **sequīre* > seguir, *tacuĭssem* > tagues̩.

1. Several words show a different development: cf. *Ltblt.*, XXIV, 335; *Zs.*, XXVIII, 381. In *aqua* (or *acqua*) and *aquĭla* (or **acquĭla*) the first consonant became, for some reason, a spirant, which later changed to i: aχwa > aiwa > aigua aiga, áχwila > áiwila > áigwila > aigla. So *aiglentina*. These same words show irregularities in other languages. Perhaps the dialect form *eigal* (Auvergne, Arles) for *egal* is to be explained in the same way; but the *ei* here may be analogical.

2. In several words kw was reduced to c (or c') in Vulgar Latin: *coquĕre* (+ *cŏcus*) > *cŏcĕre* > cǫzer, *tŏrquēre* **tŏrquĕre* (+ **tŏrco* **tŏrcunt*) > **tŏrcĕre* > tǫrser. Cf. § 55, W.

Lw > lgw > lg: *caluit* > calc, **toluĭstī* > tolguist, *valuĭssem* > valgues̩, *vŏ̊luĕrunt* (§ 16, 2) > vǫlgron.

Nw, ngw, nkw > ngw > ng: *tĕnuit* > tęnc, **venuĭsset* > vengues̩; *sanguem* > sanc; *cīnque* (= *quinque*) > cinc.

1. Tęuns < *tĕnuis* is probably a learned word; the transposition of u and n may have been due originally to a misreading of the letters. *Ianuer*, *manual*, etc. are learned. *Maneira* is apparently from a Vulgar Latin **man(u)aria* from *manuarius*. For *enquerre* < *inquærĕre*, see § 59.

2. *Exstĭnguĕre* (+ **exstĭngo* **exstĭngunt*) > **estĭngĕre* > estẹnher.

Pw > upw > up > ub: *sapuĭsset* > saubẹs, *recĭpuit* > recẹup.

1. *Saupes* apparently belongs to a dialect in which au prevented voicing. Cf. § 65, P, 3.

Rw > rgw > rg: *mĕruit* > męrc.

Sw seems to have been reduced early to s in *consuetūdĭnem* **costūmen* > costüm (costüma). *Cōnsŭo* apparently became **cōsio*, whence an infinitive **cōsĕre* or **cosīre* (Pr. cǫzer, cosir).

Tw > dw > gw > g: *pŏtuit* > pǫc.

1. *Ba(t)tuo*, *qua(t)tuor* were reduced to *batto*, **quattor* in Vulgar Latin: Pr. *bat*, *quatre*.

5. GROUPS ENDING IN Y.

73. This class contains: 1st, combinations of consonant + y < e̯ or i̯, cf. § 40, (2); 2d, consonant + g′ > y (§ 55, G), the g′ having been in some cases always contiguous to the preceding consonant, in others originally separated from it by a vowel; 3d, consonant + g > y, the g representing an original c or g between the last two vowels of a proparoxytone, cf. § 65, G, (3). It does not include dy and gy, which early became y: see § 65, Y. The groups will be considered in alphabetical order:—

Bry > bry in *ebriăcum* > ebriac (*iure* is probably French).

*β*y was early reduced to y in *habeo habeam* etc. and *dēbeo dēbeam* etc., partly, no doubt, through the proclitic use of these words, partly under the influence of *audio* > **auyo audiam* > **auya* and *vĭdeo* > **veyo vĭdeam* > **veya*; this y, like any other medial y (§ 65, Y), became dž or remained y: ai (for some reason there seems to have been no form **ach*), aia; dẹi dẹch, dẹia. Aside from these words, *β*y > udž and uy apparently in the north; elsewhere uy, by, vy—uy prevailing in the west, by and vy in the south and east. When the y became final, it changed to i, which, after a consonant, was syllabic. Ex.: *abbrĕviat* > abrẹu̯ia, **aggrĕviat* > agrẹu̯ia, **allĕviat* > alẹu̯ia, *avĭŏlum* > aviọl ai̯ọl, *cavĕa* > gabia cau̯ia, *labia* > lavia-s, **leviarius* > leugiẹrs, **rabiam* (= *rabiem*) > rabia rau̯ia,[1] **rabiāre* > rabiar, *rabiōsus* > rabiọs rau̯iọs, *rŭbeum* > rọg rọi,[2] **sabium* > savi sabi, *atavia* > tavia, *vidŭvium* > vezọig bedọi.[2] In purely learned words, Latin *bi*, *vi*, etc., are kept: *abiurament*, *fluvial*.

Cc′y: see C′y.

---

[1] *Ratie* is perhaps French.

[2] After o, the u disappears.

Cly > l′: *coclearium* > cuilhiẹr.

Cty > is: *factiōnem* > faiṣsọ, *lectiōnem* > leissọ, *suspectiōnem* > sospeissọ. In purely learned words we find the spellings *cti*, *cci*, which doubtless indicate ktsy or ksy: *electio*, *accio*. Cf. Ssy.

C′y, cc′y, kwy > ts; this ts, when it remained medial, was reduced, before and during the literary period, to s: *bracchia* brassa, *bracchium* > bratz bras (§ 64), *faciam* > faza fassa, *faciem* > fatz fas, *glaciem* > glatz glas[1], *laqueāre* > lassar, *laqueum* > latz las, **pĕcia* > pẹssa, *placeam* > plassa. Learned words have *zi* and *ci*, doubtless pronounced at first dzi, tsi, later zi, si (cf. A. Horning, *Zs.*, XXIV, 545; XXV, 736): *iuzizi iudici*, *edifici*, *Grecia*. Cf. Pty.

D–g > dž: *jūdĭco* > iütge, *mĕdĭcum* > mẹge, **sĕdĭcum* > sẹie[2].

Dy: see § 55, Y and § 65, Y.

Gdy: see § 80, Gd.

Gy: see § 55, Y and § 65, Y.

Kwy: see Cy.

Lc′y > lts > uts > us: *calceāre* > caussar. Cf. Lty. See § 74, (2).

Lg′ apparently became ldz udz uz in **fŭlgĕrem* (= *fŭlgur*) > fọuzer.

Ll–g′ > l′ in *cŏllĭgit* > cuẹlh. Cf. Ly.

Lly: see Ly.

Lny > n′: *balneum* > banh.

Lty > lts > uts > us: **altiāre* > auçar aussar. Cf. Lc′y. See § 74, (2).

---

[1] *Glai* is due perhaps to the analogy of *ney* (§ 65, β, 3), perhaps to such double forms as *fatz fai* = *facit*.

[2] *Seti* (pronounced with two syllables) seems to be an improperly constructed post-verbal noun from *assetiar*.

Lvy>lby>uby in *salvia*>saubia (Gascon).

Ly, lly>l′: *consĭlium*>cossẹlh, *fīlium*>filh, *fīlia*>filha, *nūllī*+vowel>nülh. Learned words have *li*: *familiarmens*. *Lili liri lire*<*līlium* are doubtless learned; *lis* is French.

Mby>mby, mdž, and ndž; mdž being the usual form in the literary language: *cambiāre*>camiar caniar cambiar.

Mmy>my, mdž, and ndž: *commeātus*>comiatz coniatz.

Mny>n′ in Limousin and in the extreme east and south-west, elsewhere ndž: *somniāre*>sonhar soniar. *Somni*, beside *suenh songe*, is learned.

Mply>mply in *ampliāre*>ampliar, probably learned.

My>my and n′: *sīmia*>simia, *vindēmia*>vendẹmia vendanha.

Nc′y>nts>ns: **Francia*>Fransa. Cf. Nty.

Nd-g>ndž: **pĕndĭcat*>penia, *vĭndĭco*>vẹnie. Similarly *mandūcāre*>**mandugare manduyare mandyare*>maniar[1].

Ndy>n′: **Burgŭndia*>Borgọnha, *verecŭndia*>vergọnha. Cf. Ny.

N-g>ndž: **excommĭnĭco* (=*excommūnĭco*)>escomẹnie[1], *mŏnăchum*>monie.

Ng′>n′ and ndž: *jŭngĕre*>iọnher iọnger, *ŭngĕre*>ọnher ọnger, *plangĕre*>phanher planger, *pŭngĕre*>pọnher pọnger. *Angel* is probably learned.

Ng′y>ndž: *spŏngia*>esponia.

Nty>nts>ns: *cantiōnem*>cansọ, *comĭn(i)tiāre*>comensar, *sperantia*>esperansa. Purely learned words have *nti*: *essentia*. Cf. Nc′y.

Ny>n′: *extraneum*>estranh, *tĕneo*>tenh, *vĕniat*>venha. Before or during the literary period final n′ or n′s lost its

[1] Apparently *maniar*, *escomeniar* developed in the region where g became y before a: cf. § 65, G, (1).

palatal quality in many dialects: _ingĕnium_>genh gen. If _estraniar_ comes from _extraneāre_ (and not from *_extranicāre_), it must be a word of later adoption; so _estrangier._ In _sotran_ <_subterraneum_ there is probably a change of suffix.

Pfy seems to became f in *_kŭpphja_>cọfa.

Pry probably became regularly bry: _capreŏlum_>*cabriọl cabirọl (cabrọl seems to be a new formation from _cabra_). _Coyre_<? _cŭpreum_ is unexplained.

Pty>ts, which, when it remained medial, was reduced, before and during the literary period, to s: *_captiāre_>cassar, *_corrŭptiāre_>corrossar, _nĕptia_>nẹssa, *_nŏptias_ (§ 38, 2)> nọssas. Cf. C'y.

Py remained py in the west and a part of the south, and elsewhere became ptš, later tš: _apium_>ache api, *_apprŏpiat_ (<_prŏpe_)>aprọpcha aprọcha aprọpia, _sapiam_>sapcha sacha sapia, _sapiĕntem_>sachent sapient, _sēpia_>sẹpia. If _asabentar_, 'instruct', comes from _sapientem_, it has been influenced by sabẹr, sabẹn. _Piion_<_pipiōnem_ is French. Learned words have _pi_: _copia_; but _mancĭpium_>_mancip massip._

Rc'y>rts (>rs?): _urceŏlum_ (_Zs._, XXVI, 668)>orzọl.

Rdy>rdi in _hŏrdeum_>ọrdi.

R–g>rdž: _clĕrĭcus_>clẹries.

Rg'>rdž and rdz (>rz): _argĕntum_>argen, *_burgē(n)sis_ >borgẹs borzẹs (also _borgues_, under the influence of _borc_), _dē–ērĭgit_>dẹrs, *_dē–ēr(i)gĕre_>dẹrzer (also _derdre_: §71), _sŭrgĕre_>sọrger sọrzer, _sŭrgit_>sọrtz.

Rny>rn': _Arvĕrnium_>Alvẹrnhe.

Rr–g>rdž: *_carrĭcat_>caria.

Rry?>rdž in *_horrearium_?>orgiẹr (cf. Körting).

Rt–g>rdž and rts (>rs): *_excŏrtĭcat_>escọria escọrsa.

Rty > rts > rs: *_fortiāre_ > forsar, _tĕrtium_ > tẹrz tẹrs. _Convercio_ is learned.

Rvy > rvy rby: *_cĕrvia_ > cervia cerbia.

Ry > r′, which developed into ir when it remained medial, but became r at the end of a word[1]: *_exclariāre_ > esclairar, *_donatōria_ > donadọira, *_fĕria_ > fẹira fiẹira, _fĕriat_ > fẹira, _matĕria_ > madẹira, *_mŏriat_ > mọira, _primaria_ > premẹira premiẹira (§ 23, 1), *_punitōria_ > punidọira, _varia_ > vaira, _variāre_ > vairar; *_a(u)gūrium_ > aür, _cŏrium_ > cuẹr, *_donatōrium_ > donadọr, _impĕrium_ > empiẹr, _mĭnistĕrium_ > mestiẹr, *_mŏrio_ > mọr muẹr, _monastĕrium_ > mostiẹr (§ 45, 3), _primarius_ > premiẹrs, *_punitōrius_ > punidọrs. If the ry is preceded by au, it apparently remains unchanged: _Auriācum_ > Auriac (_Zs._, XXVII, 559). Learned words have _ri_: _bori_ > _ebŏreum_, _contrari_.

1. Adjectives in _-er_ (_-ier_) and _-or_, coming from _-arium_ and _-ōrium_, regularly have feminines in _-eira_ (_-ieira_) and _-oira_. By the analogy of the masculine, there is a feminine in _-era_ in parts of the west; by the analogy of the feminine, there is a masculine in _-eir_ in Auvergne. The i of _vair_ probably comes from the feminine _vaira_ and from the verb _vairar_. The noun _feira_ sometimes becomes _fiera_ like a feminine adjective.

Sc′y: see Ssy.

Ssy, sc′y, sty > s′, which in most of the territory became is, but in the west and the extreme east developed into i(t)š and (t)š: *_bassiāre_ > baissar baichar bachar, *_angŭstia_ > engọissa, *_ingrŏssiat_ > engruẹissa, _fascia_ > faissa, *_grassiāre_ > graissar, _pŏstea_ > puẹissas pueih püch, _ūstium_ > üis.

Sty: see Ssy.

Sy > z′, which in most of the territory became iz, but in parts of the northeast, north, and west developed into i(d)ž and (d)ž, and in some scattered dialects gave y and z: _ba-_

[1] The r remained palatal long enough to cause breaking: cf. §§ 30, 37.

sium > bais bai (§ 63), *basiare* > baisar baiiar baiar bayar basar, *quasi* + vowel > cais quaish, *camisia* (cf. *Archiv für lateinische Lexikographie*, XII, 265) > camiza, *cerĕsea* (*Einf.*, § 103) > cirẹiza ciriẹiia ceriẹya ceriẹza, *ma(n)siōnem* > maisọn maiiọn maiọn mayọ, *occasiōnem* > ochaizọ, *pre(hen)siōnem* > preisọ (cf. enpreyọna, 'imprisons'), *quĭd se* + vowel > quẹis, Ger. *sazjan* > saisir, *to(n)siōnem* > toisọ.

T–g > dž: **coratĭcum* > corage, **paratĭcum* > parage, *viaticum* > viatie.

Try apparently became ir: *atrium?* > aire, *arbĭtrium* > albire.

Tty > ts > s: **plattĕa* > plassa.

Ty > apparently t′ > d′ > generally d′z′,[1] which in most of the west and north became dz, but in the south and east developed into idz; dz and idz, when they remained medial, were reduced, before and during the literary period, to z and iz: **altĭtia* > altẹza, **bellĭtia* > belẹza, *malĭtia* > malẹza, *pigrĭtia* > perẹza, **prĕtiat* > prẹza, **rikĭtia* > riquẹza; *palatium* > palatz palaitz palais (§ 64), *pŭteum* > pọtz püis, *prĕtium* > prẹtz prẹs, *solatium* > solatz solas; *potiōnem* > pozọn poizọn, **pretiāre* > prezar, *ratiōnem* > razọ raizọn, *s(t)atiōnem* > sazọ saizọn. The forms without i prevail in the literary language, and in words in which the dz comes after the accent (especially in the ending –ẹza) they seem to have encroached largely upon the ground of the others.[2] According to some philologists, the development of ty differed according to its position before or after the accent: for a brief bibliography of the discussion,

[1] These sounds lost their palatal quality too early to cause breaking: cf. §§ 30, 37. Cf. *Einf.*, § 133.

[2] *Palaitz*, however, is used by Marcabru, A. Daniel, and P. Vidal. *Poizon* occurs in *Flamenca* and in modern Limousin (beside *pozon*), *raizo* is found in the *Boeci* and other texts.

see *Zs.*, XXVII, 689. In learned words we find *zi*, *ci*, *çi*, *ti*: *estimatio*, *iustizia* *–icia* *–ecia* *–eçia*, *natio* *nacio*, *negoci*, *servizi* *–ici* (cf. A. Horning, *Zs.*, XXIV, 545, XXV, 736).

1. *Palai* (beside *palatz* *–aitz* *–ais*) may have been made from *palais* (used by Bertran de Born and in *Flamenca*) by dropping the s which was regarded as an inflectional ending. It was perhaps influenced by such words as *bais* *bai*: cf. Sy. A clerical Latin **palasium*, however, would account, not only for *palai* *palais*, but also for French *palais* and for Italian *palagio*.

2. Modern *poijon* (Alps) and *rajo* (Limousin) have perhaps followed the analogy of such words as *maison* *maijon* *majon*: cf. Sy.

3. *Escoisson* < *excŭtiunt* seems to follow **escois* < *excŭtio*. It was perhaps influenced by *conoisson* < *co(g)nōscunt*.

4. Some of the modern western dialects have d in *radon*, *sadon*, etc. = *razo*, *sazo*, etc.

6. Groups Beginning with L, M, N, R, or S.

74. (1) Of the groups beginning with l (and not ending in l, r, w, or y), the following remained unchanged (except that c before a became tš in the north and northwest).—**lb, lc** (and llc), **lg** (llg), **lm, lp, lv**: *alba* > alba; *calcāre* > calcar, *collocāre* **colcāre* > colcar (–char); *collocare* **collogare* **colgare* > colgar; *hĕlm* > ẹlm, *ŭlmum* > ọlm; *cŏlăphum* **cŏlpum* > cọlp (κόλπος > gọlfe is unexplained); *calvum* > *calv* (= calf?), *salvāre* > salvar. **Ld, ls** (lls), **lt** (llt) were regularly unchanged except for the vocalization of the l: see below. **Lc′** (llc′) became lts, and then the l was vocalized: see below. **Lc′p** became lp in *calce* *pīsāre* > calpisar. **Lg′, llg′**, have been treated in § 73. **Lvs, lvt** became ls, lt, and then the l was vocalized: see below.

(2) L became u before the dental consonants d, s, t in most of the dialects. The vocalization seems to have begun in the 8th century and to have progressed through the literary

period and later. It is difficult to trace it, as *l* long continued to be written for u. In modern Provençal, ls remains in Languedoc, lt in Rouergue. *Auça* occurs in the *Boeci.* The l was probably first retracted, to differentiate it from the following dental; and then this velar l was opened into u. Ex.: *cal(ĭ)daria* > caudiera, *cal(ĭ)dum* > caut, *sŏl(ĭ)dum* > sọlt sọut; *falsum* > fals faus, *malos* > mals maus, *valles* > vals vaus; **fallĭta* > fauta, *mŭltum* > mọlt mọut, **tŏllĭtum* > tọlt tọut; *dŭlcem* > dọlz dọutz dọus, *pŏllĭcem* > pọutz, *salĭcem* > sautz; *calvus* > *cals caus, **vŏlvĭta* > vọlta vọuta. So **altiat* > auça aussa, **calceare* > cauçar caussar: cf. § 73, Lc'y, Lty. In dọs (=dọus) and mọt (= mọut) the ọ seems to have absorbed the u. Cf. § 65, L.

1. The final t of *molt* seems to have been lost sometimes before a consonant: hence *mul*, which before d became *mon*.

2. *Altretal* (also *autretal*) became *atretal* by dissimilation; hence we have also *atressi* for *altressi* (*autressi*). *Aital*, *aitan* seem to be made up of *tal*, *tan* with the first syllable of *aissi* (<*ac sīc*), regarded as a prefix meaning 'just'.

3. *Pallĭdus* > *palles* (through **pădillus?*).

4. *Fouzer* is from *fŭlger* or **fŭlgerem* = *fŭlgur*.

75. Of the groups beginning with m (and not ending in l, r, w, or y), the following usually remained unchanged — **mb, md, mf, mp, ms, mt**: *gamba* > gamba (if *bobansa* is from βόμβος, it is irregular); **semitarium *semidarium* > semdiẹr; *triumphāre* > triomfar; *lampas *lampa* > lampa; **camisīle?* > camsil (dialectically cansil; so Samson, Sanso); *cŏmĭtem* > comte (dialectically conte). **Mbd** shows four different developments in *ambo dŭos* > ambedọs abdọs amdọs andọs. **Mbt** apparently became nt in **cambĭtos + -ōnem* > cantọn (French?). **Mn** in the literary language generally remained unchanged (often spelled *mpn*), but in some dialects it was assimilated into nn, which was locally simplified into n: _dŏmĭna dŏmna_>dompna domna donna dona, _damnāre_> dampnar damnar dannar danar, _fēmĭna *fēmna_>fẹmna fẹnna (_feme_ is from _fémena_<_fēmĭna_),[1] _hŏmĭnem *hŏmnem_> omne (_ome_ is from _*ómene_<_hŏmĭnem_).[1] **Mnc′**>ndz nz in _*domnicĕlla_>donzẹla. **Mpt**>mt, dialectically nt: _computāre_ >comtar contar, _temptāre_>temptar tentar.

76. (1) Of the groups beginning with n (and not ending in l, r, w, or y), the following generally remained unchanged (except that c, g before a became tš, dž in the north and northeast)—**nc, nd, ng, nm, nt**: _hanka_>anca, _blank-_> blanc (-ca -cha), _franko_>franc (-ca -cha); _mandāre_> mandar, _ŭnda_>ọnda; _lŏngum_>lonc (-ga -ia), _plango_> planc, _rĭng_>rẹnc; _anĭma_>anma (also, by dissimilation, arma); _sentīre_>sentir. For _final_ **nd, nt**, see (2) below. **Nc′**>nts ns: _*francē(n)sis_>francẹs, _mancĭpium_>mansip (also massip: cf. **ns** below), _vĭncere_>vẹncer vẹnser. **Nct** became in different dialects n′ int nt ntš: _jŭnctum_>iọnh ioint iọnt iọnch, _ŭnctūra_>onchüra, _*pĭnctūra_>peintüra penchüra, _planctum_>planh planch, _sanctum_>sanh saint sant. **Ndc′** became, in different dialects, ndz (later nz), nts, ndž: _quīndĕcim_>quinze quintze quinge. **Nf** remained in some dialects, while in others it became ff, then f: _confŭndit_> confọn cofọn, _infantem_>enfant effant efant, _infĕrnum_>enfẹrn efẹrn. **Ng**>ng: _mŏnăchum *mon′gu_>mongue (_manĭcum_>margue by dissimilation). **Ns**, in learned words and new formations (see § 55, N), remained in most dialects, while in others (especially those of the centre) it became ss, then s: _consĭlium_>consẹlh cossẹlh, _in sĭmul_>ensẹm essẹm, _*insignāre_>ensenhar essenhar, _pensāre_>pensar pessar, _sen-_

1 Cf. § 49, (3).

sus > sens; for *final* **ns**, see § 63, (5). **Ntc'** > nts ns in *pantĭcem* > pansa. **Nv** remained in some dialects, while in others it became vv, then v: *convenīre* > convenir covenir. **Ndc, ndg, n–g, ng'** have been treated under § 73.

(2) Final **nd** remained as nt in the eastern and central part of the territory, became n in the west and a part of Limousin, and disappeared altogether in a part of Languedoc and Gascony: *amando* > aman, *descĕndit* > deissẹn, *grandem* > grant gran gra, *mŭndum* > mọnt mọn, *vēndit* > vẹnt bẹn, *profŭndum* > preọn, *quando* > quant quan. Final **nt** remained in most of the territory, but in a part of Languedoc and Gascony became n or disappeared: *fŏntem* > font fon fo, *mŏntem* > mont mon, *quantum* > quant quan, *vĕntum* > vent bent be.

77. Of the groups beginning with r (and not ending in l, r, w, or y), the following remained unchanged (except that c, g before a became tš, dž in the north and northeast) — **rb, rc, rd, rf, rg, rm, rn, rp, rs, rt, rv**: *barba* > barba, *cŏrbum* > cọrp, *hĕrba* > ẹrba, *ŏrbum* > ọrp; *barca* > barca, *cĭrcāre* > cercar, *clĕrĭcum* **clĕrcum* > clẹrc, *fŭrca* > fọrca fọrcha, *mercātum* > mercat; *ardĕntem* > arden, **perdūtum* > perdüt, *vĭr(ĭ)dem* > vẹrt; *ŏrphănum* > ọrfe; **carricāre* **carrigāre* **cargāre* > cargar cariar, *largum* > larc (–ga –ia), *sērĭca* **sēr'ga* > sẹrga; *ĕrēmum* > ẹrm, *fōrma* > fọrma; *hibĕrnum* > ivẹrn, *tabĕrna* > tavẹrna, *tornāre* > tornar; *wĕrpan* > guerpir; *arsum* > ars, *cŭrsum* > cọrs (for *vĕrsus* > vẹs, see § 55, R); *artem* > art, *fŏrtem* > fọrt, *mŏrtem* > mọrt; *Arvernia* > Arvernha (also, by dissimilation, Al–), *servīre* > servir. For *final* **rn, rs**, see § 63, (5); § 65, R. **Rc'** > rts rs: *parcĕre* > parcer, *parcit* > partz, **tŏrcĕre* > tọrser. **Rdc'** became, in different dialects, rdz (later rz), rts, rdž: *quatuŏrdĕcim* **quattŏrdĕcim* > quatọrze quatọrtze quatọrge. **Rdg** before a > rg, rdž: *vĭridicantem* **vĭrdigantem* > verguan verian.

Rps > rs: _*escarpsus_ (= _excerptus_) > escars. **Rtm** > rtm or rm: _fŏrti mĕnte_ > fortmen formen. **Rg′** has been treated under § 73.

78. Of the groups beginning with s (and not ending in l, r, w, or y), the following usually remained unchanged through the literary period (except that c before a became tš in the north and northeast) — **sc, sm** (ssm), **sn, sp, st**: _*bŭscum_ (? = _bŭxum_) ? > bọsc, _*lŭscum_ > lọsc, _pascha_ > pasca pascha, _pĕrsĭca pĕssĭca *pĕsca_ > pẹsca, _piscātor_ > pescaire, _piscarium_ > pesquier peschier, _prĕscan *trescāre_ > trescar; _ex-mĭttĕre *esmĭttĕre_ (§ 55, X) > esmẹtre, _pĕssĭmus_ > pẹsmes; _eleemŏsўna_ > almọsna, _asĭnum_ > asne; _expōnĕre *espōnĕre_ > espọnre, _gaspildjan_? > guespilhar; _præpŏsĭtum_ > prebọst, _trīstem_ > trist. For _final_ **scs, sts**, see 2 below. **Sc′** became, in most of the territory, is; in parts of the north and northeast, s; in the west and the extreme east, i(t)š and (t)š (cf. § 73, Ssy): _co(g)nōscĕre_ > conọisser, _crēscĕre_ > crẹisser, _ex-cĕrnĕre *escĕrnīre_ > eissernir, _*ex-cerebellāre *es-_ > esservelar, _fascem_ > fais, _nascĕre_ > naisser nasser naicher nacher, _pĭscem_ > pẹis pẹich pẹch. **Scb** became sb in _epĭscŏpus *ebĭscobus_ > bisbes. **Spm** became sm in _blasphemāre_ > blasmar. **Stg** became sg and sdž in _domesticāre *-gāre_ > domesgar domesiar. **Stm** became sm in _asthma_ > asma. For the later history of the s in all these groups, see § 65, S, 1.

1. _Prĕsbўter_ became regularly prẹstre: § 71, 1. But beside _prĕsbўter_ there existed in Vulgar Latin _prebĭter_ (_Einf._, § 140), the syllable _pres-_ being replaced by the Latin prefix _præ-_ or _pre-_, through the analogy of such words as _præbĭtor_, _præposĭtus_. From the accusative _prebĭtĕrum_ we have regularly prevẹire. Prẹire (used in _Flamenca_) seems to be a cross between prẹstre and prevẹire.

2. Final sts, in nearly all the territory, was reduced to ts: _finīstis_ > finitz, _hŏstis_ > ọz (accusative ọst), _trīstes_ > tritz (sg. trist); but sts was kept in ẹstz <_ĭstos_ and in its derivative aquẹstz. Similarly final scs was

generally reduced to cs: **bŭscus ? >* (bǫscs) bǫcs (accusative bǫsc), *quĭs-quis >* quẹcs.

3. *Conois* etc. < *co(g)nōsco* etc. (beside *conosc* etc.) are doubtless due to the second and third persons (*conoisses conois* etc.). Some of the modern eastern dialects have *-isso* corresponding to *-sca* (*freisso* etc.): this seems to indicate an old metathesis of sc in that region.

7. MISCELLANEOUS GROUPS.

79. Of the groups not yet discussed, the most important are **ct, gd, gn, ks,** which show palatalization. It is now generally assumed that the Celts, who had turned their native ct into χt, pronounced Latin ct in the same way when they learned Latin (Meyer-Lübke, *Einf.*, § 186), and likewise substituted χs for ks (Meyer-Lübke, *Gram.*, I, § 650), and probably χd, χn for gd, gn. The χ was attracted into a palatal spirant by the following dental, and the dental itself was then palatalized. Most philologists explain the development of cl, gl into l′ (cf. § 68) in a similar way. Inasmuch as Indo-European pt had also been changed to χt in Celtic, it is not unlikely that the Celts substituted χt, χs for Latin **pt, ps** in a few words; the χ replacing p may sometimes have been rounded.

1. To account for palatalization in the non-Celtic parts of southern Gaul, we may assume either that the spirant pronunciation spread from the Celtic to the other regions, or that in the latter the palatalization came about simply through the mutual attraction of the guttural and the dental.

80. The groups will now be discussed in alphabetical order: —

Bc > (*pc), ptš (before a): **reprŏb(ĭ)cat >* reprọpcha.

Brg > rg in *fabrĭca *fabrĭga >* farga.

Bs > bs in the learned words *absens, absensa.*

Bsc > sc: *obscūrus >* escürs.

Bst > st: _sŭbstat_ > sọsta.

Bt > bt, t: _subtīlem_ > sobtil sotil. See also βt below.

Bts > ts: _sŭbtus_ > sọtz.

βc > uc: *_avĭca_ *_aβca_ > auca.

βc′ > udz or uts, later uz, us: _avicĕllum_ *_aβcĕllu_ > auzęl aucęl. Cf. § 65, C′, 1.

βd > ud, in the west bd: _dēbĭtum_ *_dēβĭdu_ *_deβdu_ > dẹude, _mal'habĭtum_ *_malaβĭdu_ *_malaβdu_ > malaude; _cīvitātem_ *_cīβidāde_ *_ciβdad_ > cibdat. Cf. βt below.

βt > ut, in the west pt: _dēbĭtum_ *_dēβtu_ > dẹute dẹpte, _dŭbĭto_ *_dŭβto_ > dọute dọpte, _mal'habĭtum_ *_malaβtu_ > malaute malapte; _cīvitātem_ *_cīβtate_ > ciutat (later cieutat: § 44, 2) ciptat, *_mŏvĭta_ *_mŏβta_ > mọuta, *_remōvĭtum_ ? > remọute (_Girart_). _Depte_, _malapte_ are not confined to the west (modern Limousin _dete_, Dauphiné _malate_); they come also from Latin _dēb'tum_, _mal'hab'tum_: cf. § 47, (3).

Cc′ > its > is; in the west and the extreme east itš or tš: _ecc'hīc_ > eici eissi eichi achi.

Cm > cm, m: *_Jácomus_ > Iacmes Iames (also, perhaps borrowed, Iaumes).

C′m > iṃ or sm: _dĕcĭmum_ > dẹime dẹsme, _facĭmu(s)_ > faim. Cf. § 52, (4).

Ct > tš in most of the territory; but in the north and northeast, and in the southwest, it became, as in French, it: _coctāre_ > cochar coitar, _dīctum_ > dig dit, _factum_ > fag fait, _lacte_ > lag lait, _lĕctum_ > liẹg lẹit, _lūcta_ > lücha, _nŏctem_ > nuẹg nuẹit, _pactum-a_ > pacha, _pĕctus_ > piẹg pẹitz, _ŏcto_ > uẹich[1] uẹit. The ct of _(e–)jectāre_ > getar does not show popular treatment; the word is similarly irregular in most of the other languages.

C′t seems to give the same results as ct, namely tš and it: _dīcĭtis_ > ditz, *_explĭcitāre_ > esplechar espleitar, _facĭtis_ > faitz,

[1] The _i_ in _ueich_ seems to be merely graphic.

placĭtum > plach plait, (hence *plaieiamen*, *plaideiar*), **vŏcĭtum* (= *vacuum*) > vuẹch vọig[1] vọh (hence *voiar*; *voidar* would appear to presuppose a form *vọit).

Dc, dg: see § 73, D–g.

Dc′, in the greater part of the territory, became dz, later z; but in Auvergne and some western dialects it became ts, and in parts of the southeast and southwest it gave dž: *duŏdĕcim* **dōdĕcim* > dọze dọtze dọge, *jūdĭcem* > iütge, *radicīna* > razina, *sēdĕcim* > sẹze sẹtze sẹtge. *Iütge* may have been influenced by iütiar.

Dn developed peculiarly in *consuetūdĭnem* **costūmen* > costüm, *incūdĭnem* **inclūd–?* > enclütge.

Gd > dž and id, corresponding to the tš and it from ct: **frĭgdum* (= *frīgdum*) > frẹg frẹit (fem. frẹia frẹida). The irregularity in *amy̆gdăla* > amandola goes back to Vulgar Latin. *Frezir freizir* is perhaps from **fre(i)zar* (cf. Italian *frizzare*) < **frigdiare*.

G′d: see Yd.

Gm > m: *pigmĕntum* > pimen. *Fragment* is learned. Greek γμ became um: *phlĕgma* > flẹuma, *sagma* > sauma.

Gn > n′: *agnĕllum* > anhẹl, *pŭgnum* > pọnh. According to the rhymes, final n′ would seem to have become n in many dialects. *Stagnum* > estanc, *rēgnum* > rẹnc (also *reing*) show an early metathesis. When *gnōsco* lost its *g*, *cognōsco* became **conōsco* in popular Latin.

Gnd > n′d, later, in different dialects, ind, n′d, nd, ndž: *cŏgnĭtum* **cŏn′ĭdu* > *cọnhede *cọnhde, then cọinde, cuẹnde, cọnge. Cf. Gnt below. See § 47, 1.

Gnt > n′t, later, in different dialects, int, n′t, nt: *cŏgnĭtum* > **cŏn′ĭtu* > *cọnhete (the t being due to clerical influence) >

[1] The *i* in *voig* seems to be merely graphic.

cọinte cọnte; *dĭgnitātem* **dĭn'tāte*>denhtat. Cf. Gnd above.

Ks>is, in most of the territory; in Auvergne and in the extreme east it became itš or tš: *ac sīc*>aissi, *exāmen*>eissam eicham echam, *exĭlium*>eissilh, *exīre*>eissir eichir ichir, **exorbāre*>eissorbar, *laxat*>laissa, *uxōrem*>oisọr, *tŏxĭcum*>tuẹissec. In *essaiar*, *essemple*, *essilh*, the prefix became es– through the analogy of ex– before consonants: cf. § 55, X.

Ksc>sc; before a, in the north and northeast, stš: **laxicāre*>laschar, *toxicāre*>toscar.

Ksm>s'm, later sm: *prŏxĭmum*>prọsme pruẹsme. For the later history of the s (pruẹime), see § 65, S, 1.

Kss>is: **exser(r)āre* (*Einf.*, § 142)>eissarrar, **exsūcāre*>eissügar (*essugar* presupposes a Vulgar Latin es–: see § 55, X).

Pf>f: *sapphīrum*>safir.

Ppc>(*pc), ptš (before a): **cloppicāre*>clopchar.

Ps, in some dialects, remained unaltered; but in most of the territory it changed (through χs: § 79) to is, iš, š, s, and us; iš and š belonging especially to the west, us to the east: *capsa*>capsa caissa caisha casha, *ĭpse*>ẹps ẹis, *ĭpsa mĕnte*> epsament eissamen ichamens, *met-ĭpse*>medẹis mezẹish medẹs mezẹus, *ne-ĭpse*>neẹps nẹis nẹus. The ps forms seem to have been crowded out by the others, especially by those with is.

Pt>pt, later t (except in parts of Languedoc and Gascony); in a few words, ut, it: **accaptāre* (or **accapitāre*?)> acaptar achatar, *aptum*>apte, *adaptāre*>azautar (hence *azaut*) through *aðaχtāre (§ 79), *baptizāre*>baptegar (*g*= dž) bateiar, *capitāle*>captal catal chatal, *captīvum*>captiu catiu and more commonly caitiu chaitiu (through *caχtīβu:

§ 79), *rŭpta*>rọta, *septimāna*>septmana setmana, *sĕptem*>sẹt. *Escrich escrit* (=*scrīptum*) are probably formed on the model of *dich dit.*

Td>t (through V. L. tt): *nĭtĭdum*>nẹt, *pūtĭdum*>püt. Cf. § 47, (1).

Tn: if *renha*, 'rein', is connected with *rĕtĭne* (see Körting), it must have been influenced by *renhar*<*regnāre.*

Ts: *et sīc*, under the influence of *ac sīc*, became **ec sīc*>eissi eichi ichi.

Yd>dž and id: *cōgĭto *cōyĭdo*>cüg cüit, *cōgitāre *cōyidare*>cüiar cüidar, *rĭgĭdum *rĭyĭdu*>rẹide (§ 50, 1). *Rede* is perhaps a cross between *reide* and *rege*: § 49, (1).

FINAL CONSONANTS.

81. The only single consonants that occur in Latin at the end of a word are b, c, d, l, m, n, r, s, t. The only groups (in words preserved) are ks, nt, st.

SINGLE FINAL CONSONANTS.

82. D, n, r, t at the end of proclitics (*ad*, *in*, *per*, *et*) are really medial consonants, and must be distinguished from final n, r, t in independent words (*nōmen*, *frater*, *amat*); final d occurs only in proclitics. The consonants will be treated in alphabetical order: —

B appears as b in Iacọb, p in Iọp, both learned.

C apparently fell after all vowels in some dialects; in others it remained after back vowels, and became i after a and front vowels: *eccu'hŏc* (§ 55, W)>acọ (§ 43, 2), *ecce hŏc*>aissọ çọ sọ, *hŏc*>ọ ọc (in the literary language these two forms were differentiated in use, ọ meaning 'it', ọc meaning 'yes'); *fac*>fai, *illác* (§ 16, 4)>lai la, *ecce hac*>sai sa; *dīc*>di, *ecce hīc* > eici, *sīc* > si. Düi < *dūc* may perhaps be explained as due to the analogy of *düire* and of *fai*. Cf. § 63, (6).

D in *apud* fell early: see § 65, P, 2. In the proclitics *ad*, *quĭd*, the d disappeared before a consonant, and before a vowel became in most dialects ð > z (cf. § 65, D): a, quẹ; að az, quẹð quẹz.

L fell in *in sĭmul* > essẹm. It remained in the learned Abẹl, tribunal. It is believed by some that *sivals*, 'at least', comes from *sī vel*.

M fell in Vulgar Latin at the end of a word of more than one syllable (§ 55, M): *crēdam crēda* > cręza, *dōnum dōnu* > dọn, *fŏrtem fŏrte* > fọrt; *Adam* is learned. At the end of an independent monosyllable, it fell in some dialects and in others became n (cf. § 65, N): *jam* > ia, *rĕm* > rẹ rẹn (Marcabru uses rẹy for the rhyme), *sŭm* (verb) > sọ sọn. At the end of proclitics, m was probably kept at first before vowels and labials, while it became n before dentals, ŋ before gutturals, and disappeared before spirants; but the n forms (helped by the analogy of *en*, *non*) and those without a final consonant replaced m before vowels and partly before labials, and probably took the place of ŋ before gutturals; we find, then, sometimes m before labials, but either no consonant or n before all other sounds: *quĕm* > que, *sŭm* (verb) > sọ sọn, *sŭm* (= *sŭum*) > sọ sọn sọm, **tŭm* (= *tŭum*) > tọ tọn tọm.

N fell in Vulgar Latin at the end of a word of more than one syllable (§ 55, M): *nōmen nōme* > nọm. At the end of proclitics we generally find n before a vowel, a form without n before spirants, both forms before other consonants, but often m before a labial: *ĭn* > en (*en amar*, *en cant*), e (*e Fransa*, *e ls*), em (*em breu*); *nōn* > non (*non es*, *non ges*), no (*no falh*, *no tol*), nom (*nom plagues*).

R remained: *amātor*>amaire, *cŏr*>cọr, *marmor*>marbre (*marme* shows dissimilation), *sŏror*>sọrre (*sor* through proclitic use). So in proclitics: *per*>per, *sŭper*>sọbre.

1. A Provençal final r began to fall in the west and south in the 14th century: cf. § 65, R, 1.

S remained: *amīcus*>amics, *cŏrpus*>cọrs, *facias*>fassas, *fŏrtes*>fọrtz, *ŏpĕras*>ọbras, *sŭbtus*>sọtz. Between a palatal, or an n that did not fall, and an s, a t developed in some dialects: *annos*>anz, *fīlios*>filz; cf. § 63, (1), (8).

1. Final s began to fall or to become i in many dialects as early as the 14th century: cf. § 65, S, 1. In *mai*, beside *mais*, the fall was earlier.

2. Final ts>t, in the second person plural of verbs, in parts of Limousin and Dauphiné: *habētis*>avẹt. Cf. § 64. In all first person plural forms (except esmes) final s fell very early: *amāmus amāmu'*> amám. Cf. § 167.

3. Through the influence of such common adverbs as *entz*<*ĭntus*, *fors*<*fŏris*, *ios*<*deōrsum*, *mais*<*magis*, *mens*<*mĭnus*, *nemps*<*nĭmis*, *plus*<*plūs*, *sotz*<*sŭbtus*, *sus*<*sūrsum*, s, coming to be regarded as an adverbial ending, was often added to the suffix *-men* (*belamens*), to many other adverbs, as *ensem-s*, *era-s*, *onca-s*, *poissa-s*, and to some prepositions, as *sen-s* (cf. *tras*, *vers*, etc.). By the analogy of such double forms, we have *for*, *men* beside *fors*, *mens*.

4. *Magis*, used as a proclitic, probably became in Vulgar Latin **mais* and **mas*, whence Provençal *mais* and *mas*. For *mai*, see 1 above.

T, in independent words, fell very early, except in the preterit of verbs; there it was retained in most dialects in weak preterits of the first and third conjugations, in many dialects in weak preterits of the fourth, but disappeared in strong preterits: *amat*>ama, *cantābat*>cantava, *dar' *hat*> darạ, *dōnet*>dọn, *stat*>estạ, *partībat*>partia, *placet*>platz, *tenēr' + -ē(b)at*>tenria, *vĕnit*>ven; *donāvit*>donẹt donẹ, *vēndĭdit *vendĕdit*>vendẹt vendẹ, *partīvit partīt*>partị partịt, *placuit*>plac, *vīdit*>vi. In the proclitics *et* and **ot* (= *aut*), the t fell before consonants; before vowels it became d, which, under the influence of *ad* and *quĭd*, developed like an original d: *et*>e, eð ez; **ot*>o, oð oz; later, e and o came to be used often before vowels also.

FINAL GROUPS.

83. Ks remained in Vulgar Latin at the end of monosyllables only (§ 55, X); there it became, in Provençal, is: *rēx* >rẹis, *sĕx*>sẹis. *Grecx*, *nicx* are Latinisms.

Nt was generally reduced to n; but in the extreme north and some parts of the south the t was retained in *-ant*: *amant* >aman, *habē(b)ant*>avian aviant; *cantent*>canten; *vēndunt* >vẹndon. In some dialects the n fell after o, u (vẹndo, au); *-on* and *-o* were used concurrently by the poets.

St>s in *ĕst*>ẹs. Cf. § 28, 5.

SPORADIC CHANGE.

84. For certain consonant changes no laws have been established.[1] Some of them doubtless originate in the language of children, which is governed by principles different from those which regulate the speech of adults. Others are due to vague associations of sound or sense. Borrowed and learned words are especially exposed to such whimsical alteration.

INSERTION.

85. The insertion (or addition) of a consonant, in such cases as those mentioned below, is probably always due to some false association or wrong etymology, but the specific

---

[1] The phenomena of dissimilation have been well classified by M. Grammont in *La dissimilation consonantique dans les langues indo-européennes et dans les langues romanes*, 1895. For metathesis, see *Zs.*, XXVIII, 1.

cause often cannot be ascertained; the added consonant seems to be generally a liquid or a nasal:—

alhọnd*r*e -s < *aliŭnde*: V. L. **aliŭnder*?

co*n*si = *cossi* < *eccu' sīc*: analogy of the prefix *co- con-*. Cf. § 76, (1), nf, ns.

enc*l*utge < *incūdĭnem*: cf. French *enclume*.

e*n*gal = *egal* < *æquālem*: analogy of the prefix *e- en-*. Cf. § 76, (1), nf, ns.

ị*n*vẹrn = *ivern* < *hibĕrnum*: *hi-* mistaken for the prefix *in-*; cf. Italian *inverno*, etc.

par*v*en (hence *parvensa*) < *parĕntem* (*parēre*): analogy of *ferven*, *serven*, or of *espaven*, *espavensa*?

pe*n*chenar < *pectināre*: analogy of *pencheire*, *penchura*?

perd*r*is = *perditz* < *perdīcem*: analogy of *perdre*? Cf. French *perdrix*.

pọuze*r* = *pouze* < *pŏllĭcem*: confusion with *polgar* < *pollicāre*.

ref*r*eitọr = *refeitor* < *refectōrium*: association with *refreidar* (*freit*).

re*n*linquir = *relinquir* < *relĭnquĕre*: analogy of *e- en-*; cf. *reforsar* and French *renforcer*.

METATHESIS.

86. Metathesis is not very common in Provençal, although a few texts offer many examples; it is apparently restricted to liquids and nasals:—

cabi*r*ọl = **cabriol* < *caprĕŏlum*.

cocod*r*illa < *crocodīlum*: cf. Italian *coccodrillo*.

c*r*aba = *cabra* < *capra*.

enf*r*ondar = **enfondrar* < French *effondrer* < ? **infŭndulāre*.

esc*r*emir < *skirmôn*: cf. French *escrimer*.

esta*n*c < *stagnum*: cf. French *étang*.

estu*r*men = *estrument* < *instrumĕntum*: cf. Italian *stormento*.

fo*r*mir = *fromir* < *frumjan*: cf. French *formir*, etc.

f*r*eïr = *ferir* < *ferīre*.

g*r*ada = *garda* < **warda*.

g*r*epir = *guerpir* < *wërpan*.

lhu*n* = *nulh* < *nūllum*: analogy of *negun*.

p*r*esseguier (also *pess-*) < **prĕssega* < *pĕrsĭca*.

rẹ*n*c (also *regne*) < *rēgnum*.

t*r*ida < τίγριδα.
t*r*onar < *tonitruāre* + *thrŏnus*.
t*r*uọill < *tŏrculum*.
t*r*obar < ? *tŭrbāre*: see Körting.

1. In *ginhol* = *genolh* < *genŭcŭlum* the palatalization is shifted from the liquid to the nasal. In *lunh* = *nulh* < *nullum*, on the other hand, the palatalization remains at the end of the word, but the liquid and the nasal change places.

DISSIMILATION.

87. Dissimilation, like the other irregular phenomena, affects mainly liquids and nasals, particularly r; it is not, however, entirely confined to these classes. The two nasals, m and n, are similar enough to undergo dissimilation. Some of the cases go back to Vulgar Latin, while others are peculiar to Provençal or to Provençal and French. In the table below, a dash indicates the total disappearance of the consonant in question.

β + *β* > *β* + — (v + —): *habēbam* > **aβēa* > avia, **vivāciārium* > viacier, *vivācius* > viatz. *Vianda*, whatever its ultimate origin may be, was probably borrowed from French.

kw + **kw** > k + kw: *quīnque* > *cīnque* > cinc.

l + **l** < r + l, — + l, d + l: *calamĕllum* > calamẹl caramẹl, **umbilīcŭlum* > emborígol, *flēbīlem* > flẹble frẹble fẹble, *ŭlulāre* > ulular udolar. Perhaps püs = plüs < *plūs* is to be explained by dissimilation, occurring in such phrases as *plus larc*, *plus lonc*.

m + **m** > n + m: *memorāre* > membrar nembrar (renembransa).

m + **n** > m + r: **comīnicāre* > comenegar comergar, **indomīnicātum* > ẹndomeniat endomergat, *mancĭpium* > mansip massip marsip, *manīcum* > margue, *mŏnăchum* > mongue morgue.

n + m > r + m: *anĭma* > anma arma, * *mĭnimāre* > mermar.

n + n > n + r, r + n; ? d + n: *canŏnĭcum* > canónegue canorgue, *venēnum* > verin; *nec ūnum* > negün degün? (cf. Andalusian and Asturian *dengun*, Catalan *dingu*, apparently from *nec ūnum* + *nĭngŭlum*).

r + r > r + —, — + r, l + r: * *Bernhardum* > Bernart Bernat, *marmor* > marbre marme, *prŏprium* > prọpri prọpi; *dīe Mĕrcŭrī* (influenced by *dīe Vĕnĕris*) > dimẹrcres dimẹcres, *grandem rem* > granrę ganrę, *pr(eh)ĕndĕre* > prenre penre, *prĕsbȳter* > pręstre pęstre; *arbĭtrium* > albire, *Arvĕrnium* > Alvẹrnhe, *peregrīnus* > *pele(g)rīnus* > peleris, *pŭrpŭra* > pọlpra.

s + s > — + s: * *spasmāre* > (espasme) pasmar (cf. French *pâmer*), perhaps through confusion of the initial es– with the prefix ex–.

t + t? > — + t: *statiōnem*? > sazọ (cf. French *saison*, Spanish *sazon*.

y + y > y + —: * *disjejūnāre* > * *disieunāre* > * *disy'nāre* > dis'nar disnar.

III. MORPHOLOGY.

88. The most important morphological developments are common to all, or nearly all, the Romance languages. They may therefore be ascribed, in their early stages, to Vulgar Latin, although direct evidence of their beginnings is scanty.

1. DECLENSION.

NOUNS.

89. (1) During the late Vulgar Latin and early Romance period neuter nouns gradually became masculine; this change was doubtless due in part to phonetic developments which obliterated distinctive endings: *dōnum* > dọn, m.; *nōmen* > nọm, m. *Mare*, however, became almost always feminine in Gaul: la mar. Some neuter plurals in *-a*, used mainly in a collective sense, were preserved and eventually became feminine singulars: *fŏlium fŏlia* > fọlha, f. sg.; *lĭgnum lĭgna* > lẹnha, f. sg.; so luọgua, pọma, prada, beside lọc, pọm, prat (and, by analogy, grasa, beside gras < *gradus*); similarly *labia* > lavias, f. pl.

(2) Masculine and feminine nouns usually kept their original gender. Abstract nouns in *-or*, however, regularly became feminine in Gaul, other abstract nouns being mostly feminine in Latin: *honōrem* > onọr, f.; *sapōrem* > sabọr, f. With the exception of *manus*, which generally retained its gender, feminine nouns of the second and fourth declensions, unless they

passed into the first declension (*pĭrus* > pẹra), became masculine, to conform to the usual *-us* type: *fraxĭnus* > fraisnes, m.; *pīnus* > pins, m. Attracted by such words as these, *arbor* became masculine. There were some other less important shifts.

1. *Juventus*, passing into the second declension, became masculine (*ioven*); but we find also *ioventut*, f. *Laus* became masculine in Provençal; *fin*, on the other hand, is always feminine. *Mĕrŭla* > *merle*, m. *Correitz*, *linh*, both m., occur beside *correia* < *corrĭgia*, *linha* < *līnea*. Other similar changes might be noted. Pr. *dia* (also *di*), like Latin *dīes*, is usually masculine.

90. Some nouns passed from the fourth to the second declension in the classic Latin period (*dŏmus*, *fīcus*); the rest doubtless followed in Vulgar Latin (*frūctus*,[1] *gradus*, *manus*). Fifth declension nouns in *-ies* went over, for the most part, to the first declension:[2] *dīes* > dia, *facies* > fassa, *glacies* > glassa, *rabies* > rabia; but we find also di, fatz, glatz (ratge is probably French), following the third declension type. Fifth declension nouns which did not shift to the first came to be declined after the model of the third (*fides*, *res*, *spes*). The five declensions were therefore reduced to three, presumably in Vulgar Latin times. Among these there were some exchanges: polvera, vergena; cf. § 89, (1), (2), 1.

91. The use of cases became more and more restricted in Vulgar Latin, prepositional constructions taking the place of pure case distinction. At the beginning of the Romance period, nouns probably had, in unstudied speech, only two cases in constant use: a nominative and an accusative or accusative-ablative. These two cases were generally retained

---

[1] Cato uses *fructi*.

[2] The process began in classic Latin: *materies materia*, etc.

in Provençal, for the second and third declensions, until the literary period: we may call them *nominative* and *objective*.

(1) The locative, which had almost vanished in classic Latin, lingered in Vulgar Latin only in names of places. It has left no sure traces in Provençal.

(2) The vocative, in classic Latin, was like the nominative for most words; in Vulgar Latin it probably disappeared, except in Church phrases, such as *mī dŏmĭne*. In Provençal we find the nominative regularly used in address (chanzọs, companh, emperaire, ioglars, Papiols), although the objective occasionally occurs in its stead (barọns pl., ioglar malastrüc, trachọr).

(3) The genitive, in the popular language, was little by little replaced by other constructions — commonly by the ablative with *de* or by the dative; the beginnings of this substitution may be observed as early as Plautus. Among Provençal nouns — aside from such learned forms as ancianọr, christianọr, companhọr, paianọr, parentọr — we find remnants of the genitive only in a few compound words, as diiọus < *dīe Jŏvis*, and in the standing phrase ẹs mestiẹr < *est ministĕrii.*

(4) The dative, which in most words had the same ending as the ablative, came to be replaced, in the greater part of the Empire, by the accusative with *ad*; this construction, too, goes back as far as Plautus. Provençal nouns retain no traces of the dative.

(5) The ablative, after the fall of final m (§ 55, M) and the loss of quantitive distinctions in unstressed syllables (§ 21), differed little or not at all from the accusative in the singular of nearly all nouns: *causăm causā*, *dōnŭm dōnō*, *patrĕm patrĕ*, *frūctŭm frūctū*, *dīĕm dīē.* Furthermore, some prepositions (especially *in*) were used both with the accusative and

with the ablative. It was inevitable, then, that the two cases should be confounded in the singular, and we have evidence of such confusion as early as the first century of our era; this led gradually to a substitution of the accusative for the ablative in the plural, the accusative plural being somewhat commoner and frequently simpler than the ablative. We may, therefore, take the accusative as the basis of the Provençal objective, remembering, however, that this accusative has been more or less blended with the ablative.

(6) The two-case declension remained theoretically in use in Provençal literature through the 14th century; but in texts later than the 12th, cases are often confused. From the spoken language the declension disappeared, in the west (as in Catalan), before the literary period; in the centre and east, probably in the 12th century; in the north, in the 13th. The case preserved was usually the objective, but sometimes the nominative. Some nouns in *-aire -ador* kept both forms, with a differentiation of meaning.

92. In the discussion of declensions some phonetic peculiarities must not be overlooked: —

(1) In the nom. pl. of the 2d declension, a stressed ẹ, followed in the next syllable by final -ị, would regularly give ị (cf. § 27, 1); but the ẹ is preserved by the analogy of the nom. and obj. sg. and the obj. pl.: *capĭllī* > cabẹl, *mĭssī* > mẹs, *quētī* > quẹt, *sērī* > sẹr. We do, however, find cabil, and (perhaps by analogy) auzil < *aucĕllī*.

(2) In the nom. pl. of the 2d declension, a c or g before the final -ị would regularly be palatalized (cf. § 55, C, G); but it is preserved from palatalization by the analogy of the other three forms: *amīcī* > amic, *lŏngī* > lonc.

(3) For the development of a t between a palatal or an n and a final s, see § 82, S: *annos* > anz, *fīlios* > filz.

(4) For the simplification of final scs, sts to cs, ts, see § 78, 2: **bŭscus?* > bọcs, *trīstes* > tritz.

(5) For the history of *-arius* and *-tōrius*, see § 23, 1 and § 73, Ry, 1.

93. (1) Nouns whose objective singular ended in s were invariable in the earlier part of the literary period; *bracchium* > bratz, *cŏrpus* > cọrs, *imperatrīcem* > emperairitz, *fascem* > fais, *latus* > latz, *lūcem* > lütz, *mĭssum* > mẹs, *nasum* > nas, *ŏpus* > ọps, *ŭrsum* > ọrs, *pĭscem* > pẹis, *pĕctus* > pẹitz, *prĕtium* > prẹtz, *tĕmpus* > tems, *vĕrsum* > vẹrs, *vīsum* > vis, *vōcem* > vọtz. Later, however, a plural (originally obj. pl.) was made for such words by adding -es, generally at a time when final ts had been reduced to s (§ 64): brasses, cọrses, mẹsses, pẹisses, vẹrses; examples occur as early as the end of the 12th century.

(2) Other invariable nouns are midons, sidons, and often laus and rẹs; the last two sometimes have an objective lau, rẹ. Midons comes from the Church Latin *mī dŏmĭne*, which was popularized by the substitution of the Provençal don for *dŏmĭne* and the addition of the nom. -s; the term was transferred from religious to feudal, and thence to amatory use, and came to mean 'my lady.' Sidons is formed on the model of midons.

(3) For nouns in tš, see § 63, (1): **disdūctum* > desdüg, *frūctum* > früch, *gaudium* > gaug, *nŏctem* > nuech. Such words were very often written in the plural with *-gz*, which was pronounced either ts or tš. The pronunciation ts is attested by such rhymes as *malfagz*: *alumenatz*.

94. Infinitives used substantively conformed to the 2d declension type: lauzars lauzar (like fọcs fọc), rire–s rire (like fabre–s fabre): see § 96. The same thing is true of masculine post-verbal nouns: (getar) gẹtz gẹt, (guidar) guitz guit, (lansar) lans (invariable).

FIRST DECLENSION.

95. This declension came to include a part of the fifth and also some neuter plurals of the second and third. With the exception of dia (nearly always masculine) and of a few learned words, it contained only feminine nouns. As the nominative, accusative, and ablative singular early became identical, leaving only one form in the singular, the plural forms were reduced to one, the accusative crowding out the nominative; this substitution, which must have been begun before the Provençal period, was doubtless helped by the identity of nominative and accusative plural in feminine nouns of the third declension. *Causa* will serve as a model:—

causa > causa	*causæ* **causas* > causas
causam > causa	*causas* > causas

1. *Dia* sometimes has a nom. sg. *dias*, following the example of other masculine nouns.

2. Many feminine proper names, in Gaul and elsewhere, developed a Low Latin declension *–a –āne(m)* or *–a –ēne(m)*, as *Anna Annāne*. Provençal has few traces of this inflection. The word *putana* < ? *pūtĭda* + *ānem* + *a* may be a remnant of it. Cf. Meyer-Lübke, *Gram.*, II, p. 27; E. Philipon, *Les accusatifs en* –on *et en* –ain, *Rom.*, XXXI, 201.

SECOND DECLENSION.

96. This declension came to include the fourth. With the exception of mas, 'hand' (generally feminine), it contained only masculine nouns. The different types may be illustrated by *fŏcus*, *dōnum*, *faber*:—

fŏcus	> fǫcs	*dōnum* **dōnus*	> dǫns	*faber*	> faure fabre fabres
fŏcum	> fǫc	*dōnum*	> dǫn	*fabrum*	> fabre
fŏcī	> fǫc	*dōna* **dōnī*	> dǫn	*fabrī*	> fabre
fŏcos	> fǫcs	*dōna* **dōnos*	> dǫns	*fabros*	> fabres

For the c of *fŏcī*, see § 92, (2). For **dōnus*, etc., see § 89 (1). Nom. fabre is due to the analogy of the other three cases; the s of fabres is borrowed from the prevailing fǫcs type.

1. Neuters which long preserved their gender often have no *-s* in the nom. sg.: *segle* or *segles*. Nouns in *-age* from *-aticum* commonly have no *-s*: *corage*, *damnage*, *message*, *senhorage*; but forms with *-s* occur also. Learned nouns in *-i* from *-ium* regularly have no *-s*: *breviari*, *emperi*, *iuzizi*, *testimoni*. Post-verbal nouns, on the other hand, usually take the nom. -s: *albires*, *blasme-s*, *consires*, *desires* (cf. § 94). By the analogy of the *fabre-s*, *segle-s*, *blasme-s* types, many masculines in *-e* sometimes drop the *-s*: *clergue-s*, *diable-s*, *morgue-s*, *oncle-s*, *poble-s*. *Maestre*, *prestre* regularly have no *-s*.

2. Most proper names are declined like common nouns: *Arnautz Arnaut*, *Boecis Boeci*, *Enrics Enric*, *Lozoics Lozoic*, *Peire-s Peire*. Many proper names, however, developed in Gaul and elsewhere, from the 9th century on, a Low Latin declension *-us -ōne(m)*, as *Petrus Petrōnis* (cf. § 95, 2): hence *Carle-s Carló*, *Peire-s Peiró*, etc.; so *Bergonhs Bergonhó*, etc.

3. *Mas*, being usually feminine, has a nom. pl. *mas*.

4. For *pagadi*, *salvi*, *soli*, etc., see § 51, 1.

THIRD DECLENSION.

97. This declension absorbed a part of the fifth: cf. § 90.

98. Nouns whose stem was different in the nominative and the accusative singular, reconstructed the nominative to correspond to the accusative, the new form being similar to the original genitive: *papĭlio papiliōnem* > *papiliōnis papiliōnem*, *pēs pĕdem* > *pĕdis pĕdem*. The change began in the Vulgar Latin period. Exceptions to the rule are names of persons,

unless they ended in *–ans* or *–ens*: *nĕpos nepōtem* > nẹps nebọt; but *amans amantem* > **amantis amantem* > amáns amán.

1. *Carnis* for *caro* is used by classic writers. *Grūis* for *grūs* occurs in the *Appendix Probi* III, belonging perhaps to the 3d century. *Papiliōnis*, *pĕdis*, *travis* = *trabs*, and some others are found in the 8th century *Glossary of Reichenau.*

99. Masculine nouns of the third declension, early in the Provençal period, made their nominative plural conform to the second declension type, thus distinguishing it from the objective plural: *pater patrem patres patres* > paire paire paire paires (cf. Old French and Italian). Feminines, on the other hand, kept the nominative plural in –s: *mater matrem matres matres* > maire maire maires maires.

100. A few neuter nouns, becoming masculine in Vulgar Latin, developed distinctively masculine forms in the singular: *gĕnus gĕnus* > **gĕnĕris* **gĕnĕrem* > genres genre; so *fŭlgur* (> *fŭlger*) > **fŭlgĕrem* > fọuzer. Most neuters, however, kept in the singular their original stem: *sēmen* > sẹm, *tĕmpus* > tems. But those in *–men* regularly, and those in *–r* sometimes, took an –s in the nominative singular: *flūmen flūmen* > flüms flüm, *marmor marmor* > marme–s marme; cọr, in the literary language, usually has no nominative –s. In the plural most neuters brought their forms into harmony with the masculine type, but those in *–us* kept the –s throughout: (*caput* >) *capus* **capum capĭta capĭta* > caps cap cap caps, *cŏr cŏr cŏrda cŏrda* > cọr cọr cọr cọrs, *nōmen nōmen nōmĭna nōmĭna* > nọms nọm nọm nọms; but *cŏrpus cŏrpus cŏrpŏra cŏrpŏra* > cọrs cọrs cọrs cọrs. *Mare*, becoming feminine, was declined thus: mars mar mars mars.

1. *Gĕnus* also became *ges*, which was used as an adverb.

101. The third declension comprises three principal types: (1) nouns which in Latin had no difference of stem or of accent between the nominative and the accusative singular; (2) those which had a difference of stem but not of accent; (3) those which had a difference of accent.

(1) Nouns with no difference of stem or of accent:—

MASCULINE

canis > cas	*pater* > paire-s	*sōl* > sọl-s
canem > ca	*patrem* > paire	*sōlem* > sọl
canes > ca	*patres* > paire	*sōles* > sọl
canes > cas	*patres* > paires	*sōles* > sọls

FEMININE

fīnis[1] > fis	*mater* > maire	*fĭdes* > fẹs
fīnem > fi	*matrem* > maire	*fĭdem* > fẹ
fīnes > fis	*matres* > maires	*fĭdes* > fẹs
fīnes > fis	*matres* > maires	*fĭdes* > fẹs

1. Masculine nouns of this type which etymologically had no -s in the nom. sg., often took one, even in the earliest times.

2. *Laus* and *res* were often invariable, but were sometimes declined like *sols* and *fes*.

(2) Nouns with a difference of stem but not of accent:—

MASCULINE	FEMININE	NEUTER
*pōns *pŏntis* > ponz	*pars *partis* > partz	*lūmen* > lüm-s
pŏntem > pon	*partem* > part	*lūmen* > lüm
pŏntes > pon	*partes* > partz	*lūmĭna* > lüm
pŏntes > ponz	*partes* > partz	*lūmĭna* > lüms

NAMES OF PERSONS

cŏmes > coms	*hŏmo* > om
cŏmĭtem > comte	*hŏmĭnem* > ome omne[2]
cŏmĭtes > comte	*hŏmĭnes* > ome omne
cŏmĭtes > comtes	*hŏmĭnes* > omes omnes

1. For other neuter types, see § 100.

2. *Om* later developed an inflection *oms om om oms*.

3. *Lex*, *rex* became *leis lei leis leis*, *reis rei rei reis*.

---

[1] See § 89, 1.

[2] See § 47, (3).

(3) Nouns with a difference of accent: —

MASCULINE		FEMININE	
*sĕrmo *sermōnis*	> sermọs	*ratio *ratiōnis*	> razọs
sermōnem	> sermọ	*ratiōnem*	> razọ
sermōnes	> sermọ	*ratiōnes*	> razọs
sermōnes	> sermọs	*ratiōnes*	> razọs

NAMES OF PERSONS IN -ANS, -ENS

*amans *amantis*	> amáns	*parens *parĕntis*	> paréns
amantem	> amán	*parĕntem*	> parén
amantes	> amán (*f.* amáns)	*parĕntes*	> parén (*f.* paréns)
amantes	> amáns	*parĕntes*	> paréns

NAMES OF PERSONS NOT IN -ANS, -ENS

amātor	> amaire	*sĕnior*	> sẹnher	*mŭlier*	> mọlher
amatōrem	> amadọr	*seniōrem*	> senhọr	*muliĕrem*[1]	> molhẹr
amatōres	> amadọr	*seniōres*	> senhọr	*muliĕres*	> molhẹrs
amatōres	> amadọrs	*seniōres*	> senhọrs	*muliĕres*	> molhẹrs
servītor	> servire	*baro*	> bar	*sŏror*	> sọrre sọr[2]
servitōrem	> servidọr	*barōnem*	> barọ	*sorōrem*	> sorọr
servitōres	> servidọr	*barōnes*	> barọ	*sorōres*	> sorọrs
servitōres	> servidọrs	*barōnes*	> barọs	*sorōres*	> sorọrs

1. After the same pattern as *senher*, we have *pastor pastōrem* > *pastre pastór*, etc.; after the *bar* pattern, **companio* (*Einf.*, § 43) **companiōnem* > *companh companhó*, **fĭllo* (Körting) **fillōnem* ? > *fel feló*, *glŭtto* (= *glūto*) *gluttōnem* > *glot glotó*, *latro latrōnem* > *laire lairó*, *lĕo* (treated like the name of a person) *leōnem* > *leu leó*, etc. On the model of *amaire*, *servire*, we find *trobaire trobadór*, etc., *iauzire iauzidór*, etc.; and, for the second and third conjugations, *teneire tenedór*, etc., *beveire bevedór*, etc. The inflection of such words became much confused, and some of them eventually developed double declensions: *bars bar bar bars*, *barós baró baró barós*; *emperaires emperaire emperaire emperaires*, *emperadórs emperadór emperadór emperadórs*. Some proper names follow the *bar* model: *Bret Bretó*, *Folc-s* (*Folques*) *Folcó* (later *Folcós Folcó*), *Gasc Gascó*, *Uc Ugó*, (later *Ucs Uc*); cf. § 96, 2.

[1] See § 16, 1.
[2] See § 52, (1), 1.

ADJECTIVES.

102. What has been said concerning the inflection of nouns applies also to adjectives: see §§ 91–101. For pronominal adjectives see §§ 114 ff.

1. The operation of phonetic laws sometimes results in a difference in stem between the m. and the f.: *bos bona, larcs larga, nutz nuda, preon preonda*; *mut muda, prezat prezada.* For *pauc pauca, rauc rauca,* see § 65, C, 1. For *-arius -aria, -ōrius -ōria,* see § 23, 1; § 73, Ry, 1.

2. Adjectives in -s or -š are undeclinable in the m. sg.: *glorios, perfieg.* Those in -s originally had no inflectional ending in the m. pl., but later they sometimes added -es: *divers diverses, frances franceses.* For the pl. of those in š, see § 93, (3).

103. We must recognize two classes of adjectives: (1) those which in Latin distinguish the feminine from the masculine; (2) those which do not.

1. Adjectives like *acer*, which, though inflected after the 3d declension type, could distinguish the m. from the f. in the nom. sg., fell into one or the other — usually the first — of the following classes (*agre agra, alegre alegra; terrestre terrestre*).

(1) Masculine and feminine different: —

MASCULINE		FEMININE	
bĕllus	> bęls	*bĕlla*	> bęla
bĕllum	> bęl	*bĕllam*	> bęla
bĕlli	> bęl	*bĕllæ* * *bĕllas*	> bęlas
bĕllos	> bęls	*bĕllas*	> bęlas
pauper	> paubre-s	*paupĕra*	> paubra
paupĕrum	> paubre	*paupĕram*	> paubra
paupĕri	> paubre	*paupĕræ-*as*	> paubras
paupĕros	> paubres	*paupĕras*	> paubras

(2) Masculine and feminine alike: —

MASCULINE		FEMININE	
fidēlis	> fezẹls	*fidēlis*	> fezẹls
fidēlem	> fezẹl	*fidēlem*	> fezẹl
fidēles	> fezẹl	*fidēles*	> fezẹls
fidēles	> fezẹls	*fidēles*	> fezẹls

1. Some adjectives of the second class were attracted into the first either in Vulgar Latin or in Provençal; this happened to all adjectives in *-és*, *-able*, *- ible*, and also to *comun*, *dous*, *fol*, *freble*, *graile*, *len*, *mol*, *noble*, *paubre* (early), *rude*, *trist*: *cortes cortesa*, *durable durabla*; *comuna*, *doussa*, etc. Some kept both inflections: *dolens*, *dolens* or *dolenta*; *grans*, *grans* or *granda*, etc. So *gens*, *gens* or *genta*.

104. In impersonal constructions we frequently find a nominative singular without -s, which is apparently a survival of the Latin neuter: *m'es bel* (*greu*, *parven*, *semblan*, etc.) *que* . . . But the form with -s sometimes occurs in the same constructions: *m'es greus que . . .*

1. For *es mestier*, see § 91, (3).

105. Most adverbs of manner were formed by adding -men (-ment, -mens, or -menz) to the feminine singular of the adjective: belamen. These adverbs were originally ablative phrases: *serēna mĕnte*, etc. In Provençal the specific meaning of the -men was forgotten, but the two parts might still be separated by an intervening word: ẹpsa . . . ment. When two adverbs in -men were used together, the ending was generally affixed to only one, oftener the first. Bona and mala could be used as adverbs without the suffix.

1. For the adverbial ending -s, see § 82, S, 3.

COMPARISON.

106. Adjectives and adverbs regularly formed their comparative by prefixing plüs to the positive, and their superlative by prefixing the definite article to the comparative: cara, plüs cara, la plüs cara. This method of comparison goes back to Vulgar Latin times.

1. 'Than' is expressed by *que* and *de*.

107. Some adjectives preserved their old comparative in

–ior. These comparatives had an inflection similar to that of sẹnher: cf. § 101, (3) and § 101, (3), 1.

POSITIVE		COMPARATIVE	
altus:	aut	——	aussọr
**bellātus* = *bĕllus*:	——	bellaire bellázer–s	bellazọr
gĕnĭtus:	gen	génser–s	gensọr
**grĕvis* = *gravis*:	gręu	gręuger	——
grŏssus:	grǫs	gruęysser	——
laiδ:	lai	láiger	
largus:	larc	——	largọr
lĕvis:	lęu	lęuger	——
lŏngus:	lonc	——	lonhọr
(*grandis*):	(gran)	máier	maiọr
(*bŏnus*):	(bon)	męlher	melhọr
(*paucus*):	(pauc)	mẹnre–s	menọr
nūgālis:	——	——	nüalhọr
(*malus*):	(mal)	pẹier	peiọr
(*mŭltus*):	(mọlt)	——	plüsọr[1]
sŏrdĭdus:	sorde	sordẹier	sordeiọr

108. The following neuter comparatives were used as adverbs: gensẹis gensẹs gensẹtz (< génser influenced by longẹis, sordẹis); longẹis longẹitz < ? *longĭtius (< longĭter + lŏngius); mais < *magis*; męlhs < *mĕlius*; mẹns < *mĭnus*; pẹitz < *pĕjus*; sordẹis < *sordĭdius*; viatz < *vivacius*. Mais, męlhs, mẹns, pẹitz were used also as neuter pronouns. Viatz lost its comparative sense.

109. A few adjectives, most or all of them learned, preserved the old superlative form with an intensive sense: altisme, carisme, pęsme, prǫsme, santisme.

---

1 Perhaps from a fusion of *plūs* and *pluriōres* = *plūres*. Cf. Fr.

NUMERALS.

110. The cardinal numerals are: —

ün	ǫnze	vint e ün	dozent
dǫs	dǫtze	vint e dǫs	tresent
tręs	trętze	trẹnta	quatre cen
quatre	quatǫrze	quaranta	cinc cens (de)
cinc	quinze	cinquanta	mil
sęis	sętze, sędze	sessanta	dǫs milia
sęt	dętz e sęt	setanta	tręs melia
uęg	dętz e uęg	quatre vint	quatre mila
nǫu	dętz e nǫu	nonanta	cinc milliẹrs (de)
dętz	vint, vin	cent, cen	cent miria

111. The first two numbers were inflected as follows: —

u(n)s üna	düi dǫi	dǫas dǫs
ü(n) üna	dǫs (düi)	dǫas dǫs

Düi dǫi are from Vulgar Latin *dŭī* = *dŭo*; dǫs is from *dŭos*, dǫas from *dŭas*. Tręs has a form trẹi (originally nom. m.), patterned after düi, and a form trẹis, which seems to be a cross between tręs and trẹi. For the dialect forms of ǫnze–sętze, see §76, (1), Ndc′, and §80, Dc′. Cen, multiplied by another number, took a plural form when used substantively; when used adjectively, it generally did not, but we find dozentas with a feminine noun. Mil had four plurals, milia miria melia mila; milliẹrs is a noun.

1. As an example of a longer compound numeral, we have *cen e quatre vint e ueg*.

2. From *ambo* we have the obj. forms, m. and f., *ams*, *ambas*. *Ambo* combined with *dŭī* (*dŭos dŭas*), and perhaps influenced by Pr. *ab* (§ 65, P, 2), had this inflection:

amdui	*andui*	*abdui*	*ambedui*	*amdoas*
amdos	*andos*	*abdos*	*ambedos*	*amdoas*

112. The ordinal numerals had separate forms for the two genders; the masculine forms followed the second declension type, the feminine forms, the first declension. After 5th, they were made by adding to the cardinal numeral the originally distributive ending *–ēnus –ēna.*

primiẹr, primiẹra	seizẹ(n), seizẹna	onzẹ(n), onzẹna
segọn(t), segọnda	setẹ(n), setẹna	dozẹ(n), dozẹna
tẹrz, tẹrza	ochẹ(n), ochẹna	vintẹ(n), vintẹna
quart, quarta	novẹ(n), novẹna	centẹ(n), centẹna
quint, quinta	dezẹ(n), dezẹna	milẹ(n), milẹna

113. Beside primiẹr we find premiẹr prümiẹr promiẹr (§ 44, 1, 3), and also prim and primeiran; for the developments of the ending –iẹr, see § 23, 1 and § 73, Ry, 1. Tẹrz, tẹrza regularly became tẹrs, tẹrsa (§ 83, Rty). Such forms as segọnda, tẹrcia, sẹxta, octava, nọna, dẹcima are learned.

1. As an example of a compound ordinal numeral, we have *vintena tersa.*

PRONOUNS.

114. Under this head will be treated not only pronouns and pronominal adjectives, but also articles.

115. In popular Latin the personal, possessive, and demonstrative pronouns and adjectives had two sets of forms, according as they were accented or unaccented (§ 19). *Ille,* when stressed and used pronominally, became a disjunctive personal pronoun of the third person; when unstressed and used pronominally, it furnished the conjunctive forms of the third person; when unstressed and used adjectively, it developed into a definite article. *Ipse* had similar uses. These differentiations must have begun in Vulgar Latin times.

116. The declension of *ĭlle* was considerably altered in Vulgar Latin. The neuter *ĭllud* disappeared, being replaced by *ĭllum.* Through the influence of *quī cūjus cūī,* **ĭllī illū-*

jus[1] *illūī*[1] came to be used beside *ĭlle illīus ĭllī.* The feminine had, beside *illīus ĭllī*, a genitive and dative *ĭllæ*; through the analogy of *illūjus illūī*, *ĭllæ* was expanded into *illæjus*[1] *illæi.*[1] *Illīus* then went out of use. In the plural, *illōrum* (which in some regions, by the analogy of *illūjus illūī*, had a form **illūrum*) crowded out *illārum*; this *illōrum* came to be used also as a dative.

Ipse and *ĭste* followed in the main the same course as *ĭlle.*

ARTICLES.

117. The indefinite article comes from *ūnus*, which seems to have been occasionally so used even in classic Latin: —

ü(n)s	üna
ü(n)	üna

118. (1) The definite article comes from unaccented *ĭlle*, which, being used as a proclitic, regularly lost its first syllable (§ 19). *Ille* (**ĭllī*), *ĭllum*, *ĭllī*, *ĭllos*, *ĭlla*, *ĭllas* became respectively le (li), lo, li or lhi,[2] los, la, las. Le, lo, li, lhi, la frequently elided their vowel before another vowel (l'an, l'arma), becoming l or lh. Furthermore, le, lo, li, lhi, los, in the intertonic position after a vowel (vé lo páire), regularly lost their vowel (vẹl páire)[3]; and, by analogy, la and las were sometimes reduced to l and ls. We have, then, beside the full forms, the proclitics l, lh, and the enclitics l, lh, ls. Inasmuch as l might be vocalized before a dental,[4] the enclitics l and ls sometimes became u and us (a͡u portẹr, e͡uz dias antix).

(2) The particles e and que, with the enclitic l, formed

[1] These forms existed as early as the 1st century of our era. See *Zs.*, XXVI, 600, 619. *Ejus*, *ei* may have had some influence.

[2] See § 67, (2).

[3] § 45.

[4] § 74, (2).

combinations ẹl and quẹl. Quẹl, being understood as *qu'el*, gave rise to a form ẹl.

(3) In the f. nom. sg. there is a form li or lhi, which is hard to explain. The most likely theory is that when the masculine *quī* took the place of the feminine *quæ* (see § 133), the masculine **ĭllī* came to be used beside *ĭlla*,[1] for the feminine. The Provençal feminine li (lhi) which resulted was strongly supported by the analogy of a feminine possessive mi, beside ma (see § 127).[2]

(4) The regular forms are, therefore, the following: —

		MASCULINE				FEMININE			
Sg.	*nom.*:	lẹ	li	l	ẹl	la	li	lhi	l	lh
	obj.:	lọ	l	u	ẹl	la	l			
Pl.	*nom.*:	li	lhi	l	lh	las				
	obj.:	lọs	ls	us		las	ls			

In many texts the objective forms lo, los, ls are used in the nominative.

1. The m. obj. sg. *le*, obj. pl. *les*, which occur in a few texts, are doubtless French. So is the enclitic form *s* for *ls* or *us*: *de s*, *entre s*, *e s*.

2. The enclitic forms combine as follows with the prepositions *a*, *con*, *de*, *en*, *entre*, *iosta*, *per*, *sus*, and with the conjunctions *e*, *ni*, *o*, *que*, *si*: *al au als aus*, *col*, *del deu dels deus* (*des*), *enl el els eus*, *entrels*, *iostal*, *pel pels*, *sul suls*; *eil* (= *e lhi*) *el* (= *e lo*), *nils*, *oill* (= *o lhi*), *quel*, *sil*. They combine freely with other words: *eral* (= *era le*), *fals* (= *fa los*), etc.

119. In some southwestern and some southeastern dialects we find forms sọ, sọs, sa, sas, coming from *ĭpse*.

PERSONAL PRONOUNS.[3]

120. In Vulgar Latin *ĕgo* lost its *g* (§ 55, G). The dative,

---

[1] Cf. Meyer-Lübke, *Gram.*, II, p. 104.

[2] See Suchier in *Grundriss*, I, p. 627.

[3] Cf. A. von Elsner, *Ueber Form und Verwendung des Personalpronomens im Altprovenzalischen*, 1886.

mĭhi, was preserved only in its contracted form, *mī*. After the pattern of *mī*, **tī* and **sī* were created for the other persons.

121. Provençal has no nominative forms that are regularly unaccented. In the conjunctive forms of the third person (not reflexive), the direct object is distinguished from the indirect; elsewhere there is no such distinction.

CONJUNCTIVE FORMS.

122. Latin *mē*>mẹ, *mī*>mi, *nōs*>nọs; *tē*>tẹ, **tī*>ti, *vōs*>vọs; *sē*>sẹ, **sī*>si. Me mi, te ti, se si, used as proclitics before a vowel, or as enclitics after a vowel, were reduced to m, t, s: m'ama, t'apela, s'es; o͡m, be͡t, cosi͡s. Nọs and vọs, used as enclitics after a vowel, became respectively ns and us; que͡ns, no͡us; *sī vōs*>sius, later sieus (§ 32). The forms (all objective) for the first and second persons and for the third person reflexive are, then:—

	FIRST PERSON	SECOND PERSON	THIRD PERSON (REFLEXIVE)
Sg.:	mẹ mi m	tẹ ti t	sẹ si s
Pl.:	nọs ns	vọs us	sẹ si s

1. The pronouns of the first and second persons could, of course, be used reflexively.

123. The conjunctive forms of the third person (not reflexive) come in the main from the proclitic *ĭlle*: *ĭllī*, *ĭllum*, *illōrum* (**illūrum*), *ĭllos*, *ĭlla*, *ĭllas* became respectively li or lhi, lo, lọr (lür), lọs, la, las. When used proclitically or enclitically, under the conditions described in § 118, (1), li (lhi), lo, los were reduced to l (lh), l, ls; and l was sometimes vocalized. O<*hŏc* was employed also, meaning 'it.' The adverb *ĭnde* became ẹnt ẹn n (and, through the analogy of me m, te t, se s, also ne), which was often used as a pronoun with the sense 'of it', 'of them', sometimes 'of him', 'of her'; nọs ẹn > nọn, vọs ẹn > vọn. The adverb *hīc* became i, meaning 'here' or 'there,' which served also as a dative pronoun, 'to it,' 'to them'; it was then always an enclitic, forming a diphthong with a preceding vowel; it regularly took the place of li in the constructions lọi = lo li, lai = la li. The forms are:—

		MASCULINE	FEMININE	NEUTER
Sg.	*gen.*:	ẹnt ẹn n nẹ	ẹnt ẹn n nẹ	ẹnt ẹn n nẹ
	dat.:	li lhi l lh i	li lhi l lh i	i
	acc.:	lọ l u	la	lọ l ọ
Pl.	*gen.*:	ẹnt ẹn n nẹ	ẹnt ẹn n nẹ	
	dat.:	lọr lür	lọr lür	
	acc.:	lọs ls	las	

1. *Les* for *los* is doubtless French. *Los*, *ls* were occasionally used for m. *lor*; *lors*, which occurs rarely for *lor*, looks like a cross between *lor* and *los*.

2. The following combinations illustrate the use of the enclitic forms: *aura i*, *be i*, *e l*, *laissa n*, *no i*, *qui ll*, *si ls*.

DISJUNCTIVE FORMS.

124. Vulgar Latin **ĕo* or **ĕu* > ẹu iẹu (§ 30), which before an enclitic became ẹ iẹ (ẹ͡l, iẹ͡n). The other forms explain themselves. The nominative tü, from the beginning of the 13th century, was sometimes used for tẹ after prepositions; this use may have been suggested by the existence of lü = 'him'; § 125, (1). Nọs + ẹn > nọn, vọs + ẹn > vọn.

		FIRST PERSON	SECOND PERSON	THIRD PERSON (REFLEXIVE)
Sg.	*nom.*:	ẹu iẹu ẹ– iẹ–	tü	
	obj.:	mẹ mi	tẹ (ti?) tü	sẹ si
Pl.	*nom.*:	nọs	vọs	
	obj.:	nọs	vọs	sẹ si

1. We find, besides, the French or borderland forms *ie iou iu yo* for *eu* (*gi* and *iey* have been noted also), *mei tei sei* for *me te se*.

125. The disjunctive pronouns of the third person (not reflexive) come from accented *ĭlle*, with the exception of ọ from *hŏc*. *Illūi*, *illōrum*, *illæjus*, *illæi* lost their first syllable, perhaps through elision after a vowel; *illūjus* disappeared. *Ille*, **ĭllī* gave ẹl ẹlh, il ilh; ẹl sometimes vocalized its l. *Illūī* became lüi, in some dialects reduced to lü. *Illum* became ẹl ẹlh. *Illōrum* (**illūrum*) gave lọr (lür). *Illos* became ẹls (often ẹus) ẹlhs. *Illa*, *ĭllam* both gave ẹla ẹlha. *Illæjus* became lęis lięis (in some dialects reduced to lięs).[1] *Illæi* gave lęi (dialectically lę) lięi. *Illas* became ẹlas ẹlhas.

(2) In the feminine singular nominative there is, beside ẹla ẹlha, a form ilh il. This is probably to be explained, like the feminine article lhi li, as coming from the masculine nominative *ĭllī introduced into the feminine, and supported by the feminine possessive mi: see §118, (3).

(3) Some dialects preserve the final -i of ẹli (m. pl. nom.) and ilhi ili (f. sg. nom.): see §51, 1.

(4) Occasionally the conjunctive li (f. sg. obj.) and lo (neuter sg. nom.) were used as disjunctive forms. And sometimes the masculine lüi lü was used for the feminine.

(5) The forms are, therefore, the following: —

		MASCULINE	FEMININE	NEUTER
Sg.	*nom.*:	ẹl ẹu ẹlh il ilh	ẹla ẹlha ilh il ilhi ili	ẹl lọ
	obj.:	lüi lü ẹl ẹlh	lęis lięis lięs lęi lięi lę ẹla li lüi lü	ọ
Pl.	*nom.*:	il ilh ẹl ẹlh ẹli	ẹlas ẹlhas	
	obj.:	lọr lür ẹls ẹus ẹlhs	lọr lür ẹlas ẹlhas	

In many texts the objective forms ẹls ẹlhs, lęis lęi are used

[1] Cf. Thomas in *Rom.*, XII, 334; Meyer-Lübke in *Gram.*, II, page 104. For a different explanation, see Ascoli in *Archivio glottologico italiano*, XV, 314, 396.

in the nominative. We then find occasionally a new objective, ẹlses.

POSSESSIVES.

126. Beside *mĕus mĕa*, *tŭus tŭa*, *sŭus sŭa*, there existed in popular Latin the shorter forms **mĕs?* **ma*, **tŭs* **ta*, *sŭs sa*. Of the two forms *vĕster* and *vŏster*, only the latter was used. To supply the lack of a third person possessive denoting a plural possessor, *illōrum* came to be employed as a possessive.

SINGULAR POSSESSIVE.

127. (1) The primarily atonic possessives come from the shorter Latin forms. The original masculine singular forms of the first person were displaced by mọs mọ, made on the analogy of tọs tọ, sọs sọ, which come regularly from **tŭs* **tŭm*, *sŭs*, *sŭm*; so in the objective plural we find mọs, corresponding to tọs < **tōs*, sọs < *sōs*. *Mĕī*, *tŭī*, *sŭī* gave mẹi, tọi tüi, sọi süi (§34), which, however, were often replaced by the objective forms. **Ma* **mam* **mas*, **ta* **tam* **tas*, *sa sam sas* became ma mas, ta tas, sa sas; ma, ta, sa often elided their a before a vowel. The formation of *midons* has been explained in §91, (2); §93, (2); §118, (3): from it came a feminine singular possessive mi, and, by analogy, ti and si.

(2) The forms are: —

		FIRST PERSON		SECOND PERSON		THIRD PERSON	
Sg.	*nom.*:	mọs	ma mi	tọs	ta ti	sọs	sa si
	obj.:	mọ mọn	ma mi	tọ tọn	ta ti	sọ sọn	sa si
Pl.	*nom.*:	mẹi mọs	mas	tọi tüi tọs	tas	sọi süi sọs	sas
	obj.:	mọs	mas	tọs	tas	sọs	sas

They are generally used only adjectively, and without the definite article. In some early texts, however, tọs and sọs, preceded by the article, are used substantively.

128. (1) The primarily tonic possessives come from the longer Latin forms. *Mĕus mĕum mĕi mĕos*>mẹus mẹu mẹi mẹus, which regularly became miẹus etc. (§30); an analogical form miẹu is found beside miẹi. In the feminine of the first person we have, instead of *mẹa, miẹua and mia: the first of these two forms is evidently made up from the masculine; the second may be due partly to the analogy of mi, partly to a proclitic use of the word (§44, 4).[1] In the second and third persons the masculine forms are mainly, and the feminine forms partially, replaced by analogical formations based on the possessive of the first person; *tŭi*, *sŭi*, *tŭa*, *sŭa*, however, give regularly tọi tüi, sọi süi, tọa tua, sọa sua (§8).

(2) The forms follow, those of the third person (which correspond exactly to those of the second) being omitted:—

FIRST PERSON

Sg.	*nom.*:	mẹus miẹus	mia miẹua
	obj.:	mẹu miẹu	mia miẹua
Pl.	*nom.*:	mẹi miẹi miẹu	mias miẹuas
	obj.:	mẹus miẹus	mias miẹuas

SECOND PERSON

Sg.	*nom.*:	tẹus tiẹus	tọa tua tiẹua tia
	obj.:	tẹu tiẹu	tọa tua tiẹua tia
Pl.	*nom.*:	tọi tüi tẹi tiẹi tiẹu	tọas tuas tiẹuas tias
	obj.:	tẹus tiẹus	tọas tuas tiẹuas tias

They may be used adjectively or substantively, with or without the definite article.

1. We occasionally find a neuter sg. nom. form without final *-s*: *lo mieu.*

PLURAL POSSESSOR.

129. *Nŏster*, *vŏster* developed regularly after the *pauper*

[1] For a different explanation of *mia*, see *Gram.*, I, pp. 246–248; also Horning in *Zs.*, XXV, 341.

model: §103, (1). The masculine singular nominative often took an –s: cf. §96; §101, (1). Some southeastern dialects preserved the –i of nọstri: cf. §51, 1. Beside vọstra we occasionally meet vọstri, due to the analogy of feminine mi, ti, si.

		FIRST PERSON		SECOND PERSON		THIRD PERSON	
Sg.	*nom.*:	nọstre–s	nọstra[1]	vọstre–s	vọstra vọstri	lọr lür	lọr lür
	obj.:	nọstre	nọstra	vọstre	vọstra vọstri	lọr lür	lọr lür
Pl.	*nom.*:	nọstre nọstri	nọstras	vọstre	vọstras	lọr lür	lọr lür
	obj.:	nọstres	nọstras	vọstres	vọstras	lọr lür	lọr lür

These forms are used adjectively or substantively, with or without the definite article.

1. In later times *lor* came to be inflected like a one-gender adjective: § 103, (2).

DEMONSTRATIVES.

130. Latin *ĭdem* went out of use. Latin *ĭs* was preserved only in the phrase *ĭd ĭpsum* (*ad ĭd ĭpsum* > adẹs), and in the combination *ĕccum*, in which it ceased to be recognized, so that *ĕccu'* was regarded as a synonym of *ĕcce*.

131. (1) The demonstrative particles *ĕcce* and *ĕccu'* were often prefixed to pronouns in Vulgar Latin. Being thus proclitically used, they frequently lost their first syllable (§19); sometimes, however, under the influence of *ac* (as in *ac sīc* > aissi), they preserved it, assuming the vowel of *ac*: *ecce ĭlla* > aicẹla, *eccu' ĭsta* > aquẹsta; cf. §43, (2).

(2) The suffix *–met* was used in Vulgar Latin as an intensive prefix. Its change of place was probably due to such phrases as *sēmet ĭpsum*, understood as *sē metĭpsum*. The *–t*, before a vowel, regularly gives –d– (*met–ĭpsum* > medẹs); but we find, besides, –z– (< Lat. *d*), introduced perhaps through the analogy of *ĭd* in *ĭd ĭpsum* (**medĭpsum* > mezẹis); and also

–t– (< Lat. *tt*), which may be the result of a combination of *met–* and *ĭd–* (*met-ĭd-ĭpsum* > * *metdĭpsu* > metẹis).

132. The pronouns preserved, either in their simple form or combined with a prefix, are the following: —

(1) Of *hīc* only the neuter, *hŏc*, was kept. *Hŏc* > ọ; *ecce hŏc* > aiçọ aissọ, and çọ sọ; *eccu' hŏc* > aquọ acọ. All of these are invariable.

(2) *Ipse* appears as ẹps ẹpsa, ẹus ẹussa, ẹis ẹissa (with a m. pl. ẹisses and a neuter ẹis); the last forms are the commonest; for the development of the *ps*, see §79 and §80, Ps. *Met-ĭpse* gives (medips) medẹs, (metẹish) metẹis, and, more commonly, mezẹis (f. mezẹissa, neuter mezẹis); see §131, (2). **Met–ĭpsĭmus* becomes medẹsme–s, mesẹsme–s, meẹsme–s (§65, D), with feminine forms in –a. Unaccented *ĭpsum* is probably one source of the neuter sọ: cf. § 132, (1). For the article (so, sa), see §119.

(3) *Ille*, uncombined, developed into an article (§ 118) and a personal pronoun (§§ 123, 125), but went out of use as a demonstrative. Combined with *ecce* and *eccu'* it gave: aicẹl aissẹl, cẹl, sẹl; aquẹl. Echẹl (pronounced ekẹl?) seems to come from *eccu' ĭlle* with its original initial vowel preserved. *Ipse ĭlle* perhaps gave rise also to a sẹl, which ultimately coincided with the form coming from *ecce ĭlle*. There is a neuter aicelo, perhaps aicẹl + ọ. Cẹl will illustrate the inflection of all these words; the forms are to be explained like those of the disjunctive personal pronoun (§ 125): —

		MASCULINE					FEMININE				
Sg.	*nom.*:	cẹl	cẹu	cẹlh	cẹls[1]	cellüi	cẹla	cẹlha	cil	cilh	cilha[2]	
	obj.:	cẹl	cẹu	cẹlh		cellüi	cẹla	cẹlha	celẹi	celẹis	celiẹis	cilh

[1] *Cels* shows the influence of masculine nouns and adjectives.

[2] *Aquel* has also *aquilli*. *Cilha* is evidently a combination of *cilh* and *celha*.

		MASCULINE	FEMININE
Pl.	*nom.*:	cil cilh cẹlh cẹls[1]	cẹlas cẹlhas
	obj.:	cẹls cẹlhs[2]	cẹlas cẹlhas

(4) *Iste* gave ẹst, ẹstz, ẹsta, ẹstas. *Ecce ĭste* became aicẹst (not common) and cẹst sẹst; *eccu' ĭste* became aquẹst echẹst, and chẹst. Aquẹst will illustrate the inflection; the forms are to be explained like those of cẹl: —

		MASCULINE	FEMININE
Sg.	*nom.*:	aquẹst	aquẹsta aquist aquisti
	obj.:	aquẹst	aquẹsta
Pl.	*nom.*:	aquist aquisti	aquẹstas
	obj.:	aquẹstz aquẹtz	aquẹstas

INTERROGATIVES AND RELATIVES.

133. The interrogative and relative pronouns were confused and combined in Vulgar Latin, *quī* taking the place of *quĭs*, and *quĭd* gradually encroaching on *quŏd*. Furthermore, the masculine forms were used instead of the feminine, which disappeared. We have in Provençal no evidence of the survival of any other cases than the nominative, dative, and accusative singular and the nominative plural: —

		MASCULINE AND FEMININE	NEUTER
Sg.	*nom.*:	*quī* > qui	*quĭd* > que, (*before vowel*) quez
	dat.:	*cūī* > cüi	*cūī* > cüi
	acc.:	*quĕm* > que	*quĭd* > que, (*before vowel*) quez
Pl.,	*nom.*:	*quī* > qui	*quæ* > que

The distinction between que < *quĕm*, que quez < *quĭd*, and que < *quæ* could not be maintained; we have, then, simply three forms: a nom. sg. or pl. qui, a nom.-acc. sg. or pl. quẹ (quẹz), a dat. sg. or pl. cüi (sometimes written *qui*).

[1] *Aquel* has also *aqueli*.

[2] *Aquel* has also *aquelz* and *aquelses*.

134. We have also *qualis*, which came to be inflected like fezẹls: see § 103, (2); the feminine singular, however, often dropped its -s, and sometimes took the ending -a (cal, cala). *Quīnam* apparently became quina, which, understood as a feminine form, developed a masculine, quin. There seems to have been also a **quīniam* (cf. *quŏniam*?), which gave quinh, quinha. Cf. D. Behrens in the *Zeitschrift für französische Sprache*, XVII, ii, 67-8, footnote. The phrase *de ŭnde* became dọnt, dọn, which was often used with the meaning 'of which', 'of whom'.

135. (1) In Provençal the interrogative pronouns are: **qui,** 'who' or 'whom'; **que quez,** 'what'; **cüi,** 'to whom' or 'whom', 'to what' or 'what' (obj.); **cals** (either alone or preceded by the definite article, inflected as in § 134), 'which'; **quin quinh, quina quinha,** 'which'. **Cals** is used also as an adjective.

(2) The relative pronouns are: **qui,** 'one who', indefinite (used also, in early texts and in southwestern Languedoc, as the regular relative pronoun for persons); **que quez,** 'who' or 'whom', 'which'; **cüi,** 'whom', 'which' (generally used as indirect object of a verb, or after a preposition); **lo cals** (inflected as in § 134), 'who' ('whom'), 'which'; **don dont,** 'of which', 'of whom'.

INDEFINITE PRONOUNS AND ADJECTIVES.

136. The following words call for special mention:—

(1) **Alcüs** < * *alĭqu' ūnus = alĭquī ūnus*, 'someone'. Inflection: alcüs, alcü(n); alcüna.

(2) **Alquant** < *aliquantum*, *aliquanti*, 'somewhat', 'some'; diminutive, **alquantet.**

(3) **Alques alque** < *alĭquĭd*, used as an invariable neuter

pronoun or adverb, 'something', 'somewhat'. The -s form, which originally developed before a vowel, was preferred because of the analogy of other neuter pronouns and adverbs. The preservation of the e is due to association with quez que. Alque was sometimes used as an adjective.

(4) **Als al au**, used as an invariable neuter pronoun, 'something else'. Al (au) may have been detached from alques, understood as al ques. Meyer-Lübke, however, takes it, as well as Old French el, from **alum* = *aliud*: *Gram.*, II, p. 649. Als owes its -s to the analogy of other neuter pronouns, such as alques, ẹis, mais, mẹlhs, mẹns, pẹis, etc.

(5) **Altre autre** < *alter*, 'other', pronoun and adjective. A dative **altrūī*, following *illūī*, goes back to Vulgar Latin. The Provençal forms autrüs, autrü show the influence of alcüs and negüs; autri belongs to the southeastern dialects (cf. aquẹli, ẹli, nọstri, tüti, etc.). Inflection: —

		MASCULINE	FEMININE
Sg.	*nom.*:	autre autres autrüs	autra
	obj.:	autre autrüi autrü	autra
Pl.	*nom.*:	autre autri	autras
	obj.:	autres	autras

(6) **Altretals autretals** < *alter talis*; by dissimilation, **atretals**: by substitution of ai- (first syllable of aissi < *ac sīc*) for atre-, **aitals**; by fusion of aitals and atretals, **aitretals**; through analogy of atressi, **atrestals**. Cf. § 74, 2. Inflection like that of cals (§ 134).

(7) **Altretan atretan aitan atrestan** etc. < *alter* + *tantum*: see **altretals**.

(8) **Cada un** < κατά + *ūnum*, 'every one'. The Greek preposition κατά was introduced into the Latin territory, probably by Greek merchants, in stating prices: καθ' ἕνα = *cata ūnum*,

κατὰ τρεῖς = _cata trēs_; hence cada ün, cada trẹi. Inflection: cada üs, cada ü(n); cada üna.

(9) **Calacom qualacom qualaquom**, 'something', 'a little', seems to be a Provençal compound of cal and acọ (§ 132), the last syllable of which was perhaps understood as cọm cọ < _quōmŏ(do)_. Cf. **quezacom** below. There is a diminutive **calacomet**, which helped to maintain the m of calacom.

(10) **Cals que quals que, cal que qual que**, 'whoever', is a Provençal compound.

(11) **Cant quant can quan** < _quantum quanti_, 'how much', 'how many'. Cant, inflected like bę1 (§ 103), is used also as an adjective and as a masculine and feminine pronoun.

(12) **Cascüs chascüs**, 'everyone', 'every', appears to be a fusion of cada üs and *cescüs < *_cisqu' ūnus_ = _quĭsque ūnus_ = _ūnus quĭsque_. Inflection: cascüs, cascü(n); cascüna.

(13) **Ent en n ne** < _ĭnde_, 'some': cf. § 123.

(14) **Maint mant man manh** < Celtic *_mantî_, 'many', 'many a', 'many a one'. Obj. pl. in -s, f. sg. in -a, f. pl. in -as.

(15) **Molt mout mot mul mon** < _mŭltum_, 'much'. For mọt, mul, mọn, see § 74, (2) and § 74, 1. Mọlt, inflected like bęl (§ 103), is used also as an adjective and as a masculine and feminine pronoun.

(16) **Negüs** < _nĕc ūnus_, 'no one'. Inflection: negüs, negü(n); negüna. Beside negün we find **degün**, apparently through dissimilation.

(17) **Nüls** < _nūllus_, 'no', 'none'. Inflection: nüls, nül, nül nülh, nüls; nüla, nülas. From **nülh** < _nūllī_ comes a set of forms with lh: see § 67, (2). Hence, by metathesis suggested by the analogy of negün, **lhün**. A fusion of nülh and lhün results in **lünh**, whence a set of forms with nh.

(18) **Om** < _hŏmo_, 'one'.

(19) **Pauc**<*paucum*, *pauci*, 'little', 'few'. There is also a regular adjective, paucs, 'small'.

(20) **Que que**, 'whatever', is a Provençal compound.

(21) **Quecs**<*quĭsquis* (§ 78, 2), 'everyone'. From quẹcs were formed an objective quẹc and a feminine quẹga (cf. amics amic amiga).

(22) **Quesacom** (diminutive **quesacomet**), 'something', 'a little', is formed like calacọm above, the first element in this case being either quẹs<*quĭd* or quẹ s = quẹ es.

(23) **Qui que**, 'whoever', is a Provençal compound.

(24) **Res re**, 'anything', 'something.

(25) **Tals**<*talis*, 'such', inflected like cals (§ 134).

(26) **Tamanh**<*tam magnum*, 'so great'; f. tamanha.

(27) **Tant tan ta**<*tantum*, *tanti*, 'so much', 'so many'. Tant, inflected like bęl (§ 103), is used also as an adjective and as a masculine and feminine pronoun.

(28) **Totz**<*tōttus* = *tōtus* (*Gram.*, I, § 547), 'all', had a regular inflection: tọtz, tọt, tọt, tọtz; tọta, tọtas. In the masculine nominative plural, however, we find oftener the forms tüch tüich tüit tüt tüti, which point to a Latin **tŭctī* (cf. Italian *tutti*); for this no satisfactory explanation has been discovered (see Nigra, *Rom.*, XXXI, 525). Hence we occasionally have in the singular tütz, tüt, and in the objective plural tügz tütz; the last form occurs also as a nominative plural. Tọt is frequently used as a neuter pronoun and as an adverb.

(29) **Üs**, 'some'; from *ūnus*, used as an indefinite adjective or pronoun, we have the plural forms: ü(n), ü(n)s; ünas.

2. CONJUGATION.

THE FOUR CONJUGATIONS.

137. (1) In Vulgar Latin there were some shifts, the verbs of the second and third conjugations being particularly unstable: *cadĕre, capĕre, sapĕre,* for instance, often passed into the second, while *mŏvēre, rīdēre* frequently followed the third, and *mŏri, sĕqui* usually went into the fourth. *Pŏsse, vĕlle,* with the new infinitives **potēre,* **volēre,* were made to conform with more or less regularity to the second conjugation type. Beside *do, dant, sto, stant,* there came into use the forms **dao,* **daunt,* **stao,* **staunt.* Beside *facĕre* there doubtless existed a verb **fare,*[1] strongly influenced by *dare* and *stare*; the first suggestion of shortening probably came from the monosyllabic imperative singular *fac* (or *fa*[2]), which must have led to a plural **fate* beside *facĭte.* *Habēre* and *vadĕre*[2] also came under the influence of *dare* and *stare*; the former adopted, beside *habeo, habes, habet, habent,* the forms **ho,* **has,* **hat,* **hant* or **haunt.* *Vadĕre* generally lost its past tenses, which were replaced by *īre* and, in southern Gaul, by *annare.*[3]

(2) In Provençal the first conjugation was well preserved, and the fourth lost but little. The second and the third lost many verbs (especially learned words) to the fourth: delir, emplir, envazir, espandir, fugir, iauzir, merir, regir, relinquir, reluzir, vertir;[4] cọzer cozir <*consuĕre,*[5] devire devezir <*divīdĕre,* dire dir <*dīcĕre,* lẹire legir (also lire lir) <*lĕgĕre,* quẹrre querir <*quærĕre,* sẹgre seguir <*sĕqui,* tenẹr tenir[6] <*tenēre.* More-

[1] See G. Rydberg, *Le développement de* facere *dans les langues romanes,* 1893.

[2] See A. Zimmermann in *Zs.,* XXV, 735.

[3] See C. C. Rice in *Publications of the Modern Language Association of America,* XIX, 217.

[4] Cf. §138.

[5] Cf. §72, Sw.

[6] According to Raimon Vidal, a 13th century grammarian, *tenir* is French.

over, the second and third conjugations, which in Provençal differed practically only in the infinitive, were much confused: cabẹr, cazẹr, mǫrdre, rire, sabẹr; cọrre accorrẹr, mentavẹr mentaure < *mente habēre*, movẹr mǫure, quęrre querẹr, redẹbre rezemẹr < *redĭmĕre*. Uc Faidit, a 13th century grammarian, enumerates about 500 verbs in –ar, about 100 in –er and –re, and a little over 100 in –ir.

138. The inchoative ending *–scĕre* lost its original sense. The *–īsc–* type, for verbs of the fourth conjugation, was very widely extended, the *–isc–* becoming a part of the regular present stem of the fourth conjugation, and disappearing from the infinitive: *finīre*, **finīsco* > finir, finisc. The Latin *–ēsc–* type, combining with *–īre* (*dis-pigrēscĕre* > despereissir, *evanēscĕre* > envanezir[1]), produced an ending –eissir –ezir –zir, which was used in forming some new verbs: enfolezir[2] < fǫl, envelhezir < vęlh, envelzir < vil, esclarzir < clar, escürzir < escür oscür, espaorzir < paọr. The *–āsc–* and *–ōsc–* types appear only in such old verbs as *irāscĕre* > iráisser, *co(g)nōscĕre* > conọisser.[3]

139. New verbs were formed, in late Vulgar Latin and in Provençal, only in the first and fourth conjugations. The commonest suffixes were *–āre*, *–iāre*, *–icāre*, *idiāre* (< ἴζειν: §57, Z), *–īre*: **oblītāre* > oblidar, **altiāre* > aussar, **carricāre* > cargar, **werridiāre* > guerreiar, **abbellīre* > abelir. Germanic verbs generally went into the first conjugation, except those in *–jan*, most of which entered the fourth: *roubôn* > raubar (also raubir), *wîtan* > guidar; *furbjan* > forbir, *raustjan* > raustir.

---

[1] *Esvanuir* seems to come from the perfect, *evanuī*.

[2] *Enfolhetir* shows the influence of *follet*.

[3] See K. Sittl in *Archiv für lateinische Lexikographie und Grammatik*, I, 465

FUNDAMENTAL CHANGES IN INFLECTION.

140. The Latin perfect passive took the sense of a present; *amātus est*, for instance, under the influence of such phrases as *carus est*, came to mean 'he *is* loved'. This led to the establishment of an entire passive inflection made up of the perfect participle and the parts of the verb *ĕsse*; and the old passive forms were gradually abandoned, leaving no trace (save the perfect participle and possibly the gerundive) in the Romance languages. So the passive is constructed in Provençal as in French: ẹs amatz, ẹra amatz, fọ amatz, será amatz, etc.; the participle regularly agrees with the subject in gender and number. Latin deponent verbs became active: *mŏri* > morir, *sĕqui* > seguir.

141. (1) Such phrases as *ĭd habeo factum* shifted their meaning from 'I have it done', etc., to 'I have done it', etc. The Latin perfect came to be restricted to its aorist sense, and the perfect was expressed by compounds of *habēre* with the perfect participle. In the Romance languages all compound tenses were eventually formed in this way: ai cantat, avia cantat, aurai cantat, etc. In Provençal the auxiliary is sometimes ẹsser, instead of avẹr, if the main verb is reflexive, passive, or neuter; ẹsser is particularly common with neuter verbs of motion: sọi vengütz.[1] A participle used with avẹr may agree in gender and number with the direct object, if there is one: ai cantat *or* cantada la cansọ.

(2) The Latin perfect indicative continued to be used as an aorist, and is the source of the preterit in Provençal, as in

[1] For *ai estat* we sometimes find *soi agutz*. The confusion arises perhaps from the use of both *es* and *a* in the sense of 'there is': hence *es estat* = *a agut*; and by a mixture of the two, *es agut*. Cf. L. Gauchat, *Sono avuto*, in *Scritti vari di filologia* (dedicated to E. Monaci), 1901, p. 61.

the other Romance languages: *vīdī* > vi, 'I saw'. The pluperfect indicative survived in some regions; in Provençal it is used with the sense of a conditional: *fŭĕrat* > fọra, 'he would be'. The future perfect indicative and the perfect subjunctive did not remain in Provençal: *amavĕro* = aurai amat, *amavĕrim* = aia amat. The pluperfect subjunctive assumed the functions of the imperfect, which disappeared from nearly every part of the Romance territory: *audīssem* (for *audīrem*) > auzis. The perfect infinitive left no trace: *audīsse* = avẹr auzit.

142. The Latin future, which was not uniform in the four conjugations, and, in the third and fourth, was liable to confusion with the present subjunctive, was gradually replaced by various periphrastic constructions: instead of *faciam* people said *factūrus sum*, *dēbeo facĕre*, *vŏlo facĕre*, *habeo* (*ad*) *facĕre*, etc. The construction that prevailed in the greater part of the Empire was *facĕre habeo*, a combination of the infinitive with the present indicative of *habēre*. The verb *ĕsse* was the only one that ultimately retained the old future beside the new: Pr. ẹr, ẹrs, ẹr, beside serái serás será; in the plural, only serẹm, serẹtz, serán. The new composite future was occasionally used by Tertullian, St. Jerome, and St. Augustine, and became common in Italy by the 6th century.[1]

(2) As an imperfect of the future, there was evolved a combination of the infinitive and the imperfect or perfect indicative. To correspond to *dīcit quod venīre habet*, was constructed *dīxit quŏd venīre habēbat* (or *habuit*); to match *sī pŏssum, venīre habeo*, was made *sī potuĭssem, venīre habēbam* (or *habuī*). In Gaul, as in most of the Empire, only the imperfect of *habēre* was used for this purpose. Traces of such

[1] Cf. P. Thielmann, *Archiv für lateinische Lexikographie und Grammatik*, II, 48 and 157.

a construction are found as early as the 3d century. This form is generally called the *conditional*, and it existed in Provençal side by side with the conditional described in § 141, (2): sería, serías, sería, etc., beside fọra, fọras, fọra, etc. The Romance languages developed also a perfect conditional: auría agüt = 'I should have had'.

143. (1) The present participle remained in use as an adjective: *fīlias placentes* > filhas plazẹns; cf. § 101, (3). In its verbal function it was replaced by the ablative of the gerund: *vĕnit accŭrrens* > *vĕnit accŭrrendo* > ven acorrẹn. In most Provençal dialects, however, the present participle and the gerund coincided in form (*amantem* and *amando* both > amán), the gerund being distinguished from the participle only by its lack of inflection: see § 76, (2).

(2) The gerund retained only the ablative case, the use of which was considerably extended: see above. In its other cases it was replaced by the infinitive: *artem dīcendī* > *artem dīcĕre* > art de dire. The supine, too, was replaced by the infinitive: *vīsum vĕnit nōs* > *vĕnit nōs vĭdēre* > ven nọs (a) vezẹr.

INFINITIVE, PRESENT PARTICIPLE, AND GERUND.

144. The infinitive endings *-āre*, *-ēre*, *-īre* regularly became -ar, -ẹr, -ir; *-ĕre* became -re or -er: see § 48, (1) and § 52, (1). Ex.: *amāre* > amár, *vĭdēre* > vezẹr, *audīre* > auzir; *tŏllĕre* > tọlre, *nascĕre* > náisser, *dīcere* > dire dízer. For shifts of conjugation, see § 137.

1. The fourth conjugation verbs *enantir*, *gauzir*, *grazir*, *murir*, *servir* sometimes took a final *e* by the analogy of *devire* (< *divīdĕre*), *dire*, *rire*. On the other hand, *dire* occasionally lost its *-e* by the analogy of the fourth conjugation. *Lire* for *leire* (< *lĕgĕre*) is probably French, and *lir* is to be explained like *dir*.

2. *Far* beside *faire* doubtless comes from **fare*=*facĕre*: see § 137, (1). *Trar* beside *traire* (<**tragĕre*) follows *far*.

3. *Escriure* (<*scrībĕre*) sometimes became *escrire* through the analogy of *dire*.

4. Some verbs that passed from the second to the third conjugation preserved the old infinitive as a noun: *debēre*>*deure devér*, *placēre*>*plaire plazér*.

145. The endings *–antem –ando*, *–ĕntem –ĕndo* regularly became –an or –ant, –en or –ent: § 76, (2). See § 143, (1). The endings *–iĕntem –iĕndo* lost their i in Vulgar Latin (§ 40, 1), and were thus reduced to *–entem –endo*. Ex.: *amantem amando*>amán (or amánt), *vidĕntem vidĕndo*>vezén (or vezént), *credĕntem credĕndo*>crezén (or crezént); *sapiĕntem sapiĕndo*>**sapĕntem* **sapĕndo*>sabén (or sabént), *partiĕntem partiĕndo*>**partentem* **partendo*>partén (or partént). Fourth conjugation verbs which adopted the inchoative –sc– (§ 138), generally introduced it into the present participle and the gerund: florir, florissẹn. Cf. § 155. For the declension of the present participle, see § 101, (3).

PAST PARTICIPLE.

146. The Provençal past participle comes from the Latin perfect participle. It is to be noted that verbs which originally had no perfect participle were obliged to create one in order to form their compound tenses: see § 141, (1). Past participles in Provençal, when inflected, were declined like bẹl: §§ 102; 102, 1; 103, (1). See § 141, (1).

147. In the first and fourth conjugations the endings were *–ātum* and *–ītum*, which regularly became –at and –it: *cantātum*>cantát, *finītum*>fenít. The first conjugation verbs which had a form in *–ĭtum* discarded it for *–ātum*: *crepāre crĕpĭtum*=crebár crebát. On the other hand, *aperīre* and *operīre* preserved their participle in *–ĕrtum*: cubrir (<*cooperīre*), cubęrt (also cubrít); ubrír (<*aperīre* + *cooperīre*), ubęrt. By the analogy of these, sufrir (<*suffĕrre*) and ufrir (<*offĕrre*) have sufęrt (also sufrít), ufęrt. Tenẹr tenir keeps its Provençal second conjugation ending, tengüt (see § 148); and venir, following the analogy of tenir, has vengüt.

148. (1) Most Latin verbs of the second and third conjugations had no accented ending, but a few had an ending *–ūtum*, which corresponded very well to the *–ātum* and *–ītum* of the first and fourth: *arguĕre, argūtum*; *consuĕre, consūtum*; *sĕqui, secūtum*; *solvĕre, solūtum*; *volvĕre, volūtum.* This ending was considerably extended in Vulgar Latin, especially to verbs having a perfect in *–ŭī*: *habēre, habŭī, habĭtum *habūtum.* In Provençal it spread still further: cazẹr, cazęc, cazegüt. Inasmuch as it was closely associated with the perfect, it came to be attached, more and more frequently, to the stem of that tense.

(2) Of the Provençal verbs of the second and third conjugations, about half adopted the ending -üt. In some the –üt is added to the stem of the infinitive: crezüt, defendüt, escondüt, molüt, perdüt, rešemüt, respondüt, rompüt, vendüt, vezüt veüt. Most of the verbs, however, attach the –üt to the stem of the preterit; nasc, nascüt; pasc, pascüt; tems, temsüt; tesc, tescüt; venc, vencüt (from vẹnser); visc, viscüt. A few have both forms: agüt avüt; cazegüt cażüt; vengüt venüt. It is to be noted, in the case of verbs that add –üt to the preterit, that if the third person singular of the preterit ends in a voiceless consonant preceded by a vowel or l or n, that consonant is voiced in the participle: ac, agüt; bẹc, begüt; cazęc, cazegüt; conọc, conogüt; crẹc, cregüt; dẹc, degüt; elęc, elegüt; mǫc, mogüt; nǫc, nogüt; plac, plagüt; plǫc, plogüt; pǫc, pogüt; remas, remazüt; saup, saubüt; sẹc, següt; tẹnc, ten-

güt; tǫlc, tolgüt; valc, valgüt; vẹnc, vengüt (from venir); vǫlc, volgüt. Exceptions are ceupüt, saupüt (beside saubüt), and vencüt (from vẹnser): for ceupüt, saupüt, cf. § 65, P, 3; in vencüt the c was perhaps kept to distinguish the word from vengüt (venir).

(3) The other half of the second and third conjugation verbs generally preserved the old participle with no accented ending: ars, cẹing, claus, dich, düit, estrẹit, fach, iọinch, mẹs, ọnh, pǫst, prẹs, trach, etc. Some of these have also forms in -üt: defẹs defendüt, elig eslęit elegüt, escọs escondüt, mǫut molüt, nat nascüt, remas remazüt, rọt rompüt, vis vezüt. A few verbs made up new forms without a stressed ending: conquęrre, conquẹs conquis; redemer rezemer, redems (rezemüt); sọrger, sọrs; tǫlre, tǫlt tǫut; vezẹr, vist (vis vezüt veüt); vǫlvre, vǫut. *Mĭttĕre* probably had beside *mĭssum* a form **mīsum* (cf. *mīsī*); hence mẹtre, mẹs mis. By the analogy of this, prendre has beside prẹs a form pris. Ęstre borrowed estát from estar < *stare*. Escriut, from escriure, is probably influenced by the infinitive; escrich follows dich. So, probably, does elig = eslęit, from elegir eslire eslir.

1. For sọi agütz (= ai estat), which is found not only in some Provençal dialects, but also in southeastern France, French Switzerland, and parts of northern Italy, see § 141, (1), footnote 1.

FUTURE AND NEW CONDITIONAL.

149. For the formation of these parts, see § 142, (1), (2). Ex.: amarái, creisserái, florirái. Verbs of the second conjugation regularly, and verbs of the fourth very often, syncopate the e or i of the infinitive: remanrái, volrás; partrái, venría. Third conjugation infinitives with final e drop this e before the ending; those in -er keep the e: vẹndre, vendrái; náisser, naisserái. First conjugation infinitives regularly keep the a

(§ 45), but in a few texts (especially the *Girart* and the *Rasos de trobar*) the a is changed to e: cantarái, sonaría, trobarẹm; blasmerán, comterá.

1. *Esser* keeps the old future forms *er*, *ers*, *er*, beside *serái*, *serás*, *será* (*serém*, *serétz*, *serán*).

150. For the phonetic changes exemplified in a*u*ría, de*u*rái, mo*u*rá; pla*i*ría; ca*i*rá, ve*i*rái; val*d*rái; reman*d*rém, ten*d*ría; po*i*ría, see § 70, βr, C'r, Dr, Lr, Nr, Tr. Anar (<*annāre*) has beside anarái a form irái from ir (<*īre*). Ẹsser drops its first syllable (serái), perhaps through elision (tu 'sserás, etc.), perhaps in accordance with the general principle stated in § 19. Faire far always makes its future and conditional from the latter form (farái). Sabẹr has beside sabrái a form saubrái, due no doubt to the combined influence of aurái and the preterit saup<*sapuit*. Vezẹr, following the analogy of beurái, deurái, viurái, has veurái beside the regular veirái.

151. The composite nature of the future and conditional was still sufficiently felt, in the literary period, to admit of the separation of the component parts: amar vos ái, dar n'ẹtz, donar lo t'ái, tornar nos ẹm, tornar s'en ía.

FUTURE ENDINGS.

152. For the 1st pers. sg., the Provençal verb used the form **ayo*>ai (§ 73, βy); for the 2d and 3d pers. sg. and the 3d pers. pl., the forms **has*>as, **hat*>a (§ 82, T), **hant* **haunt*>an aun (§ 83, Nt): see § 137, (1). In the 1st and 2d pers. pl., *habēmu'* (§ 82, S, 2), *habētis* naturally gave avẹm, avẹtz (§ 64); but inasmuch as the other four terminations were monosyllabic, the av– was dropped when avẹm, avẹtz came to be understood merely as future endings. The future is, therefore, inflected as follows:—

cantar–ái	cantar–ẹm
cantar–ás	cantar–ẹtz, –ẹs, –ẹt
cantar–á	cantar–án, –ánt, –áun, –áu

1. In Gascony and Languedoc we find –ẹi for –ai: see §§23, 2; 162, (4). In Gascon and in the modern dialects of some other regions –am is used for ẹm. In some dialects of Béarn, Languedoc, Provence, and Dauphiné, –ẹm becomes –ẹn: cf. § 65, M, 1; also § 167, 2.

CONDITIONAL ENDINGS.

153. *Habēbam* > aβẹβa > (probably through dissimilation: § 87, β) aβẹa > avía (§ 26); so avías, avía, aviám, aviátz, avían. But inasmuch as the conditional was formed in imitation of the future, and none of the future forms retained the av–, the conditional endings were reduced to –ía, –ías, –ía, –iám, –iátz, –ían. Some dialects, which substituted –on for –an, introduced –íon into the conditional: § 169. The conditional is, therefore, inflected as follows:—

cantar–ía	cantar–iám
cantar–ías	cantar–iátz, –iás, –iát
cantar–ía	cantar–ían, –íon, –ío

1. In verse these endings are sometimes counted as monosyllabic: poiri͡a. Guiraut Riquier uses –íatz for –iátz. In some dialects of Béarn, Languedoc, Provence, and Dauphiné, –iám becomes –ián: cf. § 65, M, 1; also § 167, 2.

PRESENT.

154. The personal endings will be discussed separately in §§ 164–169.

155. The Provençal present indicative and subjunctive come, in the main, directly from the corresponding parts of the Latin verb:—

amo > am	*amāmu'* > amám	*faciam* > fassa	*faciāmu'* > fassám
amas > amas	*amātis* > amátz	*facias* > fassas	*faciātis* > fassátz
amat > ama	*amant* > áman	*faciat* > fassa	*faciant* > fássan

In the 4th conjugation, however, most verbs have adopted the originally inchoative -sc- (§ 138) and incorporated it into the inflection of the present, except in the 1st and 2d pers. pl. of the indicative:—

florisco	> florísc	*florēmu'*	> florẹm[1]
florīscis	> florís florísses	*florētis*	> florẹtz[1]
florīscit	> florís	*florīscunt*	> floríscon
florīscam	> florísca	*floriscāmu'*	> floriscám
florīscas	> floríscas	*floriscātis*	> floriscátz
florīscat	> florísca	*florīscant*	> floríscan

We occasionally find such forms as florissẹm, florissẹtz, and florám, florátz.

1. The s coming from sc' was of course originally palatal; it is sometimes written *sh*. The sc of the 1st pers. sg., the 3d pers. pl., and the whole pres. subjunctive was replaced, in some dialects, by s or sh: floris florish, florisson florishon, florissa florisha.

156. Of the Latin imperative forms, only the present active, 2d pers. sg. and pl., remained in use. The Provençal verb kept the sg., but substituted for the pl. the 2d pers. pl. of the present indicative:—

ama	> ama	*tĕne*	> ten	*crēde*	> crẹ
amāte amātis	> amátz	*tenēte tenētis*	> tenẹtz	*crēdĭte *crēdītis*[2]	> crezẹtz

partī	> part	*fīnīsce*	> finís
partīte partītis	> partẹtz[2]	*fīnīte fīnītis*	> finẹtz[2]

In negative commands the present subjunctive is generally used instead of the plural imperative, and sometimes the infinitive is employed instead of sg. or pl. The verbs auzir, avẹr, dire, ẹsser, sabẹr, vezẹr, volẹr regularly took their imperative forms from the present subjunctive: áuias, digátz, veiátz, etc.

[1] For the accented vowels in these forms, see §§ 167, 168.

[2] See § 168.

1 *Fait* < *facĭte* (beside *faitz*) seems to come directly from the Latin form.

2. Before *vos* the pl. drops final *-tz* (or *-t*?): *departe vos*, *vene vos*. *Ve vos* becomes *veus*; a fusion of *ve vos* and *ec* < *eccum* results in *vecvos*.

DOUBLE STEMS.

157. Differences in accentuation and in the environment of vowels or consonants regularly developed different stems in different parts of some verbs. For instance, *ádjūtáre* > aidar (§ 45), while *adjū́tat* > aiüda.

158. Sometimes, as above, an intertonic vowel disappeared: *mándūcáre* > maniar, *mandūco* > *mandüc manüc; **parabolāre* **páraulåre* > parlar, **parabŏlat* **paraulat* > paraula. In such cases the shortened stem usually prevailed: mania, parla. But in *adjutare* the longer one was preferred: aiüdar.

159. (1) A vowel which breaks in one part of a verb may be unstressed, and therefore remain unbroken, in another part: *probāre* > proar, *prŏbat* > prueva,[3] **sequīre* > sẹguir, **sĕquit* > siẹc.[4] In such cases the phonetic development is generally undisturbed.

(2) A vowel which breaks in one part of a verb may, with different environment, remain unbroken even in another part in which it is stressed: **volēre* > volẹr, **vŏleo* > vuelh, **vŏlet* > vọl. If the breaking occurs in the 1st pers. sg., the phonetic development is regularly undisturbed; if it occurs in the 2d and 3d pers. sg., it is generally carried into the other forms in which the vowel is stressed: *cŏllĭgit* > cuẹlh, hence cuẹlh = *collĭgo*; *ĕxit* > iẹis, hence iẹsc, iẹscon, iẹsca.

160. A consonant may be followed by e̯ or i̯, and so pala-

[3] See § 37. [4] See § 30.

talized, in one part of the verb, and not in another: **cadeo* > chai, **cadēmu'* > chazẹm; *dēbeo* > dẹch dẹi (§ 73, βy), *dēbet* > dẹu; *faciat* > fassa, *facĕre* > faire; *fŭgio* > füi, *fugĕre* > fugir; *jaceam* > iassa, *jacēre* > iazẹr[1]; *placeāmu'* > plassám, *placēmu'* > plazẹm; *sapiam* > sapcha, *sapit* > sap; *tĕneo* > tenh, *tĕnet* > ten; *valeo* > valh, *vales* > vals; *vĕniat* > venha, *venīre* > venir; *vĭdeam* > vẹia, *vidētis* > vezẹtz; **vŏleo* > vuẹlh, **vŏlet* > vọl. Verbs in *-eo* generally keep this distinction; but we find mọva, somóna, tẹma = *mŏveam*, *submŏneam*, *tĭmeam*. Most verbs in *-io*, on the other hand, dropped the i̯ in Vulgar Latin: *partio* **parto* > part, *partiunt* **partunt* > parton, *partiam* **partam* > parta; sen, senton, senta; siẹrf, siẹrvon, siẹrva; etc. A few verbs show forms both with and without the e̯ or i̯: *audio* > auch (*audiam* > auia), **audo* > au; *crēdo* > crẹ, **crēdeo* > crẹi[2]; *vĭdeo* > vẹi[2], **vĭdo* > vẹ.

161. Verbs in -ng- naturally developed a palatal consonant before e or i (§ 73, Ng′), but not before other vowels: *cĭngĕre* > cẹnher, *cĭngo* > cẹnc, *cĭngit* > cẹnh, *cĭngam* > cẹnga; so fẹnher, ọnher, plánher, pọnher, etc. The palatal was carried by analogy into the parts that were originally without it: hence the double forms cẹnc cẹnh, cẹngon cẹnhon, cẹnga cẹnha, etc. These double forms led tenẹr, venir to adopt tenc, venc, tenga, venga, beside the regular tenh, venh, tenha, venha. Such forms as these, supported by dẹrc < *de-ērĭgo*, dic < *dīco*, prẹc < *prĕco*, sẹc < **sequo*, trac < **trago*, etc., afforded a starting-point for an ending -c, adopted by some other verbs in the 1st pers. sg. of the present indicative: *pĕrdo* < pẹrt pẹrc, *pr(eh)ĕndo* > pren prenc, *remaneo* > remanh remanc, etc.

---

[1] Also, by analogy, *iassér*.

[2] Raimon Vidal says that *crei*, *vei* are the proper forms for the 1st pers. sg. of the pres. indicative.

PECULIAR FORMS.

162. The following verbs have individual peculiarities that call for special mention:—

(1) **Anar** (<*annāre*), 'to go', takes most of its present from *vadĕre*: indicative, *vau vauc* (analogy of *estau estauc*), *vas*, *va vai* (analogy of *fai*), *anám*, *anátz*, *van vaun* (analogy of *estan estaun*); subjunctive, *an* or *vaza* (<*vadam*) *vaia* (analogy of *vai* and of *traia*), *vaga* (analogy of *traga*), etc.; imperative, *vai* (analogy of *fai*), *anátz*.

(2) **Aucire** (<*occīdĕre*: § 43) has in the pres. indicative 3d sg. *auci* (<*occīdit*) and *aucis* (analogy of *aucizém*, *aucizétz*). Cf. *auzir*, *caire*, *rire*, *traire*, *vezér*. These forms were doubtless helped by the analogy of *ditz* (<*dīcit*), *dütz*, *fatz*, *iatz*, *letz* (<*lĭcet*), *platz*, *tatz*.

(3) **Auzir** (<*audīre*) has in the pres. indicative 3d sg. *au* (<*audit*) and *aus* (analogy of *auzém*, *auzétz*). Cf. *aucire*, *caire*, *rire*, *traire*, *vezér*. See also § 160.

(4) **Aver** (<*habēre*) has in the pres. indicative: *ai* (<*habeo*: § 73, βy), *as*, *a*, *avém*, *avétz* (see §§ 167, 168), *an aun*; see § 137, (1). There is no trace of **ho*. Instead of *ai*, the dialects of Aude, Tarn, Tarn et Garonne, and Haute-Garonne have *ei* (cf. *Gram.*, II, p. 304), which probably developed first in the future (§ 152, 1) through the analogy of the preterit ending *-ei* which took the place of *-ai*: *amāvi* **amai*>**amai amei* (§ 175), then *amarai*>*amarei*, then *ai*>*ei*. The pres. subjunctive is *aia* (<*habeam*: § 73, βy). For the imperative, see § 156.

(5) **Caire cazér** (<*cadĕre* **cadēre*) has in the pres. indicative 3d sg. *ca* (<*cadit*) *cai* (analogy of *brai*<**bragit*, *fai*, *trai*<**tragit*, *vai*) *cas* (analogy of *cazém*, *cazétz*: cf. *aucire*, *auzir*, *rire*, *traire*, *vezér*).

(6) **Conóisser** (<*cognōscĕre*) has in the pres. indicative 1st sg. *conosc* (<*cognōsco*) and *conóis* (analogy of 2d and 3d sg., *conóisses*, *conóis*).

(7) **Creire** (<*crēdĕre*): pres. subjunctive *creza* (<*crēdam*) and *crega* (analogy of *diga*, *prega*, *sega*, *traga*). See also § 160.

(8) **Créisser** (<*crēscĕre*): pres. subjunctive *cresca* (<*crēscam*) and *crega* (analogy of *diga*, *prega*, *sega*, *traga*, and of the imperfect subjunctive *cregués*).

(9) **Dar** (<*dare*): *dau* (<**dao*), *daun* (<**daunt*); see § 137, (1).

(10) **Destruire** (<**destrūgĕre* = *destruĕre*): analogy of *agĕre*, *tĕgĕre*, etc. Cf. *traire*. **Destrūgit*>*destrüi*.

(11) **Dever** (<*debēre*) has in the pres. indicative 1st sg., beside *dech dei* (§ 160), *dec* (analogy of *dic*, *prec*, *sec*, *trac*, and perhaps of the preterit *dec*).

(12) **Dire** (<*dīcĕre*): *dic* (<*dīco*) *diu* (cf. § 51, 3; § 65, G, 1); *ditz* (<*dīcit*) *di* (analogy of *fai*, *trai*, and of imperative *di*<*dīc*); *dízon* (analogy of *ditz*, *dizém*, *dizétz*); *diga dia* (both <*dīcam*: § 65, G). For the imperative, see § 156.

(13) **Düire** (<*dūcĕre*): *dütz* (<*dūcit*) *düi* (analogy of *destrüi*, *trai*).

(14) **Eissir** (<*exīre*): *iesc*, *iescon*, *iesca*, analogy of *conosc*, *florisc*, etc.; for vowel, see § 159, (2).

(15) **Ésser estre** (<**ĕssĕre* = *ĕsse*). Pres. indicative: *sŭm* > sọn sọ (§ 82, M), then, by the analogy of *ai* and *füi*, sọi süi; *ĕs* became ẹst iẹst, perhaps through *ĕs tu* > ẹs-t-u > ẹst-tü, supported by the analogy of the preterit ending of the 2d sg. (vọs vendẹtz, tü vendẹst or vendiẹst, so, to match vọs ẹtz, a form tü ẹst or iẹst); *ĕst* became ẹs, probably through such combinations as quẹ's (understood as qu'ẹs); *sĭmu'*, which existed in Latin beside *sŭmus* (*Rom.*, XXI, 347), gave sẹm, while from *ĕstis* there was constructed an **ĕsmus* > ẹsmes (rare), and from ẹtz a form ẹm (very common); *ĕstis* > ẹstz ẹtz (§ 78, 2); *sŭnt* > sọn sọ (§ 83, Nt). Pres. subjunctive: *sīm*, *sīs*, etc., were replaced in V. L. by **sīam*, **sīas*, etc. (on the analogy of *fiam*, *faciam*, etc.), which gave sía sías sía siám siátz, sían síon; we find also sẹia, etc., formed apparently on *deia*, *veia*. Imperative borrowed from subjunctive.

(16) **Estar** (<*stare*). Pres. indicative: *estáu* (<**stao*) *estáuc* (§ 161); *estás* (<*stas*); *está* (<*stat*) *estái* (analogy of *fai*, *trai*); *estám* (<*stamu'*); *estátz* (<*statis*) *estáitz* (after *faitz*); *están* (<*stant*) *estáun* (<**staunt*); see § 137, (1). Pres. subjunctive: *estía*, etc., *estéia*, etc., patterned on *sia*, *seia*; also *estéi*, perhaps a cross between *esteia* and **esté*<*stem*. Imperative: *está*, *estáitz*.

(17) **Faire far** (<*facĕre* **fare*): § 137, (1). Pres. indicative: *fatz* (<*facio*) *fau* (analogy of *dau*, *estau*) *fac fauc* (§ 161); *fas* (<**fas*); *fatz* (<*facit*) *fa* (<**fat*) *fai* (influence of *faire*, *faim*, *faitz*, and of *trai*); *faim* (<*facĭmu'*: § 167, 1) *fam* (<**famu'*) *fazém* (see *fazétz*); *faitz* (<*facĭtis*) *fatz* (<**fatis*) *fazétz* (analogy of regular verbs, *crezétz*, etc.); *fan* (<**fant*) *faun* (analogy of *daun*, *estaun*). Pres. subjunctive: *faça fassa*, etc. (<*faciam*, etc.). Imperative: *fai* (<*fac*); *fatz faitz* (borrowed from indicative) *fait* (<*facĭte*).

(18) **Iazér** (<*jacēre*), also *iassér* (influence of *ias*<*iatz*<*jacet*, and of

iassa ?): *iatz* (<*jacet*) *iai* (analogy of *fai*, *trai*); *iassa* (<*jaceam*) *iaia* (analogy of *traia*, *vaia*).

(19) **Movér móure** (<*movēre* **mŏvĕre*): *mova* (<**mŏvam* = *mŏveam*) *moga* (analogy of *traga*).

(20) **Partir** (<*partīre*): *part* (<**parto* = *partio*) *parc* (§ 161); so *parta parga*.

(21) **Perdre** (<*pĕrdĕre*): *pert perc*, *perda perga*; see § 161.

(22) **Plazér plaire** (<*placēre* **placĕre*): *platz* (<*placet*) *plai* (analogy of *fai*, *trai*); *plassa* (<*placeam*) *plaia* (analogy of *traia*, *vaia*).

(23) **Podér** (<**potēre* = *pŏsse*): see § 137, (1). Pres. indicative: *posc* (<*pŏssum* influenced by *cognōsco*) *puosc puesc* (analogy of *puoc puec* < *pŏtui*), *puecs* (?<**pots* <**pŏtsum* + *puesc*), *pois* (<**pŏsseo*); *potz* (<*pŏtes*); *pot* (<**pŏtet* = *pŏtest*); *podém* (<**potēmu'*); *podétz* (<**potētis*); *póden* (<**potent*) *pódon*, *pon* (analogy of *potz*, *pot*, and *son* < *sŭnt*). Pres. subjunctive: *posca puosca puesca* (like *posc puosc puesc*), etc.; *poissa* (<**pŏsseam*), etc.

(24) **Prendre** (*prĕndĕre* = *prehĕndĕre*) **penre** (see § 71, end): *pren* (<*prĕndo*) *prenh* (analogy of *tenh*, *venh*) *prenc* (§ 161); so *prenda prenha prenga*.

(25) **Rire** (<**rīdĕre*): *ri* (<*rīdet*) *ritz* (analogy of *rizém*, *rizétz*: cf. *aucire*, *auzir*, *caire*, *traire*, *vezér*); *ria* (<*rīdeam* ?).

(26) **Sabér** (<**sapēre*): see § 137, 1. Pres. indicative: *sai sei* (analogy of *ai ei* from *avér*); *saps*; *sap*; *sabém* (<**sapēmu'*); *sabétz* (<**sapētis*); *sáben* (<**sapent*) *sábon*. Pres. subjunctive: *sapcha* (<*sapiam*). Imperative from subjunctive.

(27) **Tazér taire** (<*tacēre* **tacĕre*): *tatz* (<*tacet*) *tai* (analogy of *taire* and of *fai*, *trai*).

(28) **Tenér** (<*tenēre*): *tenh* (<*tĕneo*) *tenc* (§ 161); so *tenha tenga*.

(29) **Traire** (<**tragĕre*, perhaps also **tracĕre*, = *trahĕre*): *trac* (<**trago* or **traco*) *trai* (§ 63, 6)[1]; *trai* (<**tragit*) *tra* (analogy of *da*, *esta*, *fa*, *va*) *tratz* (<**tracit* ?: cf. *aucire*, *auzir*, *caire*, *rire*, *vezér*); *trázon* (analogy of *tratz*); *traga traia* (both <**tragam*).

(30) **Vezér** (<*vidēre*): *vei* (<*vĭdeo*) *vec* (§ 161); *ve* (<*vĭdet*) *ves* (analogy of *vezém*, *vezétz*: cf. *aucire*, *auzir*, *caire*, *rire*, *traire*). Imperative from subjunctive.

---

[1] According to Raimon Vidal, *trac* is the only correct form.

(31) **Volér** (< **volēre* = *vĕlle*): see § 137, (1). Pres. indicative: *vuelh* (< **vŏleo*); *vols* (< **vŏles*); *vol* (< **vŏlet*); *volém* (< **volēmu'*)[1]; *volétz* (< **volētis*); *vólon* (< **vŏlent*). Pres. subjunctive: *vuelha* (< **vŏleam*), *vuelhas*, *vuelha*, *vulhám*, *vulhátz*, *vuelhan*. Imperative from subjunctive.

163. In verse the present subjunctive ending –ia sometimes counts as one syllable: si͡atz. Cf. § 153, 1.

PERSONAL ENDINGS[2].

164. (1) In the **first person singular** final *–o* and *–em* regularly disappeared: *amo* > am, *amem* > am. When, however, the *–o* or *–em* was preceded by a consonant group requiring a supporting vowel (§ 52), the ending was regularly retained as –e: *dŭbĭto* > dọpte, *sŭffĕro* > suffre, *trĕmŭlem* > tremble.

Through the analogy of ai, crẹi, dẹi, sọi, vẹi, and the 1st pers. sg. of the preterit, this –e was in the indicative generally changed at an early date to –i: **cŏpĕro* > cọbre cọbri, **opĕro* > ọbre ọbri; so *ĭmpleo* **ĭmplo* > ompli. This –i (occasionally –e) was then taken as a distinctive ending of the 1st pers. sg., and was added to many verbs that needed no supporting vowel: auzir, au auze; azorar, azọr azọri; cantar, can canti; cọrre, cọr cọrri; mẹtre, mẹt mẹti; prezar, prẹtz prẹzi; remirar, remir remire remiri; respondre, respon respondi; sentir, sen senti; vẹndre, vẹn vẹndi.

In the subjunctive, when a final vowel was required, –e was usually kept; it was also extended to some verbs that did not need it: acabe, dọne, mire, plọre. Very rarely an unnecessary –i was added instead of –e: laissar, lais laissi.

(2) The ending *–am* regularly gave –a: *audiam* > auia.

---

[1] *Volemus* occurs repeatedly in 7th century Latin.

[2] Cf. O. Schmidt, *Ueber die Endungen des Præsens im Altprovenzalischen*, 1887.

165. In the **second person singular** final *-as* regularly remained, and *-ēs* and *ĭs* became -s (or, when a supporting vowel was required, -es): *amas* > amas; *valēs* > vals, *sapĭs* > saps, *partīs* > partz; *dŭbĭtēs* > dọptes. Cf. § 82, S. Sometimes, especially in late texts, -s is expanded into -es: canz cantes, partz partes, saps sabes, vals vales; so floris florisses, etc.

Final *-a* remained, and *-ĕ* and *-ī* fell: *ama* > ama, *tĕne* > ten, *crēde* > crẹ, *partī* > part.

166. In the **third person singular** final *-at* became -a, *-ĕt* and *-ĭt* fell (but remained as -e when a supporting vowel was needed): *amat* > ama, *amet* > am, *tĕnet* > ten te, *vĕnit* > ven ve; *trĕmŭlet* > tremble. Cf. § 82, T.

167. In the **first person plural** the final *-s* disappeared early, *s* being perhaps regarded as a distinctively second person ending[1]. The rare form ẹsmes = *sŭmus* is the only one that retains the *s*: cf. § 162, (15).

Then *-āmu'*, *-ēmu'* gave regularly -am, -ẹm: *cantāmus* > cantám, *habēmus* > avẹm. Likewise *-ĭmu'*, through the analogy of *-āmu'*, *-ēmu'*, came to take the accent on its penult, and then regularly developed into -ẹm: *crēdĭmus* **credímu'* > crezẹm. This -ẹm of the second and third conjugations passed into the fourth, and entirely displaced the -im that would have been the regular representative of *-īmu'*: *partīmus* > *partím partẹm.

1. In *faim* < *facĭmu'* the old accentuation apparently survives: cf. § 52, (4), 1.

2. In some dialects of Béarn, Languedoc, Provence, and Dauphiné, *-m* apparently becomes *-n*: *devén*, *havén*, *volén*; so *aurián*, *trobarén*, *segrián* (cf. § 152, 1; § 153, 1). Cf. § 65, M, 1.

[1] The loss of *-s* is not confined to the Provençal territory: it occurs also in western France, Catalonia, and the Engadine.

168. In the **second person plural** *–ātis* regularly gave –atz: *amātis*>amatz, *audiātis*>auiatz. The regular form from *–ētis* is –ẹtz, which we find kept in the future (veirẹtz) and in the present subjunctive (cantẹtz); in the present indicative it was replaced by –ętz, probably through the analogy of ętz <*ĕstis*: *habētis*>avętz avẹtz, **potētis*>podętz podẹtz, so sezętz, valętz, etc.; the rare avẹtz and podẹtz are the only forms that preserve ẹ. The ending *–ĭtis*, taking the accent on its penult (cf. § 167), became *–ẹtz, then –ętz: *crēdĭtis*> crezętz. This –ętz also displaced the –itz that would have been regular in the fourth conjugation: *partītis*>partętz.

The final –tz was reduced, in some of the principal dialects, to –s (§ 64): cantás, sezęs, partęs. In other dialects it was replaced very early by –t (§ 64): auiát, avęt, passát, podęt; so partirẹt, etc.

1. In *faitz*<*facĭtis* the old accentuation apparently survives.

169. In the **third person plural** *–ant*, *–ent*, *–unt* gave respectively –an –ant, –en, –on –o (§ 83, Nt): *amant*>áman ámant, *audiant*>áuian áuiant; *valent*>válen, *ament*>ámen; *vēndunt*>vẹndon vẹndo. In Languedoc –an was replaced by –on or –o in the 13th century; in other regions, later: ámon, chanto ls, coménso l. The *Boeci* has –en for –an: amen, monten. In Gascony and some of the Limousin territory –en partially displaced –on (floríssen, párten, vẹnden), elsewhere –on or –o displaced –en (válon).

IMPERFECT INDICATIVE.

170. In the first conjugation *–abam* regularly gave *–ava*. In the second, through the analogy of *aβéa*<*habēbam* (§ 153), *–ēbam* came to be replaced, in southern Gaul, by *–éa*, which regularly changed to *–ía* (§ 26). In the third, *–iēbam* regularly became *-ēbam* (§ 40, 1); and this and original *-ēbam* were replaced by the *-éa* > *-ía* of the second conjugation. In the fourth, *-ībam*, which had in the accented syllable the characteristic vowel of the conjugation, crowded out *-iēbam*; *-ībam* then lost its *β* through the analogy of the second and third conjugations. We have, then, in Provençal, only two sets of endings: *-áva*, etc., in the first conjugation; *-ía*, etc., in the second, third, and fourth.

amáva	vezía	fazía	partía
amávas	vezías	fazías	partías
amáva	vezía	fazía	partía
amavám	veziám	faziám	partiám
amavátz	veziátz	faziátz	partiátz
amávan	vezían	fazían	partían

1. In poetry *ia* is sometimes counted as one syllable: *avian*, *devian*.

2. For some subsequent developments of western dialects, see Meyer-Lübke, *Gram.*, II, p. 326.

3. For the personal endings, see §§ 164–169.

4. *Esser* has: ẹra, ẹras, ẹra, erám, erátz erás, ẹran ẹron ẹro.

PRETERIT, OLD CONDITIONAL, AND IMPERFECT SUBJUNCTIVE.

171. These parts are all formed from the same stem, that of the Latin perfect: cf. § 141, (2). Ex.: cantẹi, cantẹra, cantẹs; vendẹi, vendẹra, vendẹs; partí, partíra, partís; vi, vira, vis; dẹc, dẹgra, deguẹs.

PRETERIT.

172. Preterits which stress the ending throughout are called *weak*; those which do not stress the ending throughout are called *strong*: part*í*, part*ist*, part*í*, part*ím*, part*ítz*, part*íron* is weak; saup, saub*íst*, saup, saub*ém*, saub*étz*, sáub*ron* is strong. Verbs of the first and fourth conjugations regularly have weak preterits (amẹi, finí). Verbs of the second and third, with very few exceptions, originally had strong preterits (*placuī* > plac, *fēcī* > fis): many of them, however, developed weak preterits either in Vulgar Latin or in Provençal (irasquẹi, nasquẹi, tessẹi tesquẹi, visquẹi); some assumed a weak form in –í in the 1st pers. sg. (dis dissí, pris prenguí, remas remanguí, trais traguí: cf. §§ 173, 177); quẹrre, on the other hand, substituted a strong preterit (quis, etc.) for a weak one.

173. (1) Final *–ī*, in the first pers. sg., doubtless remained through the earlier stages of Provençal (*habuī* > águi, *dīxī* > díssi): cf. § 51, (2). Before it fell, it changed an accented ẹ in the preceding syllable to i (*vēnī* **vēnuī* > *vẹngui vinc): cf. § 27; occasionally, however, the ẹ was kept, through the analogy of the other persons (pris prẹs). Sometimes, instead of falling, the –i took the accent (following the analogy of the fourth conjugation) and remained: águi > ac or aguí, díssi > dis or dissí (cf. § 177).

When the –i was immediately preceded by an accented vowel, it regularly formed a diphthong with that vowel, and did not fall (*fuī* > füi): cf. § 51, (3); but –íi was simplified to –i (*partīvī partīī* > partí).

Before enclitic l, –ei –iei were often reduced to –e –ie: cantiẹ l.

(2) In the 2d pers. sg., *–stī* became –st, a preceding ẹ being changed to i (§ 27): *partīstī* > partíst, *debuīstī* > deguíst; sometimes, through the analogy of the 2d pers. pl., ẹ remains (venguẹst: cf. § 27, 2). Occasionally the final –t disappears: aniẹst aniẹs, fezíst fezís.

(3) The *–t* of the 3d pers. sg. was lost in strong preterits: *placuit* > plac, *vīdit* > vi. In weak preterits, it was retained

by most dialects after é, and by many after í: donẹt donẹ, vendẹt vendẹ; partí partít. Cf. § 82, T.

(4) In the 1st pers. pl., *-mus -mu'* (see § 167) was reduced to -m: *vīdĭmu'* > vim.

(5) The *-stis* of the 2d pers. pl. regularly became -tz (§ 78, 2), later in many dialects -s (§ 64): *debuĭstis* > deguẹtz deguẹs.

(6) The *-runt* of the 3d pers. pl. regularly gave -ron or -ro (§ 83, Nt): *partīrunt* > partíron partíro, *vīdĕrunt* > viron viro. In some dialects -en is substituted for -on: *fŭĕrunt* > fọron fọren (cf. § 169).

The *e* before *-runt*, which in classic Latin was usually long, was always short in Vulgar Latin when it was preserved at all: *amavĕrunt* > *amārunt*, *fēcĕrunt*.

WEAK PRETERITS.

174. (1) In the first and fourth conjugations we find in Latin the following endings:—

-āvī -āī -āvĭmus *-īvī -īī -īvĭmus*
-āvĭstī-āstī -āvĭstis -āstis *-īvĭstī -īstī -īvĭstis -īstis*
-āvit -aut -āvēre -āvĕrunt -ārunt *-īvit -īit -īt -īvēre -īvĕrunt -īrunt*

The popular speech preferred in every case the shortened form, and generally reduced *-āvĭmus*, *-īvĭmus* to *-āmus*, *-īmus* (in southern Gaul *-āmu'*, *-īmu'*: § 167), on the analogy of the 2d pers. sg. and pl.

(2) In the second conjugation a few verbs (*delēre*, *flēre*, *nēre*, *olēre*, *-plēre*, *viēre*) had similar endings (*delēvī*, etc.), which were doubtless contracted in like fashion in so far as these words were in common use. Most verbs of this conjugation, however, had strong preterits (*tacēre*, *tacuī*; *vidēre*, *vīdī*; etc.).

(3) The third conjugation had in classic Latin no weak endings corresponding to those of the first, second, and fourth; but the vulgar speech developed a set in the following manner. Compounds of *dare* formed their perfect in *–dĭdī* (*perdĭdī*); this *–dĭdī*, in accordance with the principle set forth in § 16, 3, came to be pronounced –dẹ́dị (*condédi*); and –dẹdị, probably through dissimilation[1], was shortened to –dẹi (**credéi*). With this form as a starting-point, a weak preterit was created on the analogy of those of the other conjugations, the endings being something like –ẹi, ẹstị, –ẹt, –ẹmus –ẹmu', –ẹstis, –ẹrunt. This inflection was probably extended to some verbs outside the *–dĕre* class (**battéi*, etc.?).

175. (1) In Provençal the weak inflection disappeared from the second conjugation, *delēre* and *–plēre* passing into the fourth, and the other weak verbs going out of use.

(2) Verbs of the fourth conjugation (except venir) all took the weak endings –í, –íst, –í, –ím, –ítz, –íron: partí, partíst, partí, partím, partítz, partíron. Irregular verbs either disappeared or became regular (*sensī* = sentí), with the exception of *venīre* > venir (vinc).[2]

(3) The new weak endings of the third conjugation developed into –ẹi, –ẹst, –ẹt, –ém, –ẹtz, –ẹron: vendẹi, vendẹst, vendẹt, vendém, vendẹtz, vendẹron. In the 1st pers. sg. the ẹ often broke (vendiẹi), and the diphthong was sometimes carried into the 2d pers. sg. (vendiẹst). These endings were considerably extended in Provençal (cazẹt, etc.), and were occasionally attached to a strong preterit stem (nasquẹt, tesquẹt, venquẹt, visquẹt). Most verbs, however, kept their

---

[1] Cf. the reduction of *habēbam* to *aβea*: § 153.

[2] *Tenér tenír* really belongs to the second conjugation.

strong preterit (mis, conọc). The *-īvī* perfect disappeared from the third conjugation: *quæsīvit*> **quæsit*> quẹs.

(4) The first conjugation discarded its own weak endings, and substituted those of the third: cantẹi cantiẹi, cantẹst cantiẹst, cantẹt, cantém, cantẹtz, cantẹron. This strange phenomenon seems to have originated as follows: *dare*, *dĕdī*> dar, dẹi; from dar the ending -ẹi was readily extended to estar (estẹi); and from these two very common verbs it spread to the whole first conjugation.

Irregular verbs (except *dare*, *stare*) either disappeared or became regular.

1. According to Meyer-Lübke, *Gram.*, II, p. 304, Latin *-ai* became by phonetic process -ẹi in Vulgar Latin, and -ẹi or -iẹi in Provençal. There seems to be no evidence to support this theory. Cf. § 23, 2.

2. In the dialects of Béarn and Catalonia the original *a* remains in some parts of the preterit.

176. A final -c, which developed in the strong *-ui* preterits (§ 184), often became attached to the 3d pers. sg. of weak preterits of the fourth conjugation: floríc, fugíc, iauzíc, partíc.[1] It was sometimes extended to other weak preterits: chantẹc, entendẹc, nasquẹc,[2] parẹc.[3] We find also a 3d pers. pl. cazẹgron, etc., and even a 1st pers. sg. ameguí, etc. In some western dialects the final -c was adopted by the whole first conjugation: donẹc, portẹc, etc.

177. Some strong preterits occasionally assumed weak endings:—

(1) In the 1st pers. sg. several verbs in -s sometimes either added an -í or shifted the stress to an originally unaccented

[1] According to Raimon Vidal, this is the regular ending of the 3d pers. sg. of the fourth conjugation.

[2] In *nasquec* the *ui* ending occurs twice.

[3] Beside parẹc, coming perhaps from a V. L. **parēvit* **parēvuit*.

final –i (cf. §§ 172, 173): dis dissí, pris presí, quis quesí, respos respozí. A few verbs in –c did the same: aic aiguí, bẹc beguí, conọc conoguí, saup saubí, vinc venguí, vọlc volguí. An ending –guí being thus established, this syllable was sometimes added to preterits not of the –c class: costrenguí, destrenguí, prenguí, remanguí, restrenguí, traguí.

(2) In the 3d pers. sg. weak endings are rare: ac aguẹt, vẹnc venguẹt.

(3) In the 3d pers. pl. the weak ending is not uncommon in –s preterits: diron dissẹron, düistrent düissẹron, mẹsdren mezẹron, prẹson presẹron, remastrent remazẹron, traissẹron. We probably have to deal here, as in (1), with a shift of accent—_dīxĕrunt_> *dísseron> dissẹron, etc.: see § 49, (2). The same thing may be true of such a form as aguẹron, beside ágron, from *_áβwerunt_ = _habuĕrunt_; such a form as visquẹron, on the other hand, is doubtless imitative.

STRONG PRETERITS.

178. (1) The reduplicative perfects were discarded in Vulgar Latin, with the exception of _dĕdi_ (and its compounds) and _stĕti_, whose reduplicative character was no longer apparent. _Cecĭdī_ became *_cadui_ or *_cadéi_; the rest either disappeared or passed into the _–sī_ class: _cucŭrrī_> *_cŭrsī_, _momŏrdī_ > *_mŏrsī_, _pepĕndī_> *_pē(n)sī_, _pupŭgī_> *_punsī_, _tetĕndī_> *_tē(n)sī_, _tetĕgī_> *_taxī_ *_tanxī_.

(2) The _–i_ perfects were greatly reduced in number in Vulgar Latin. Some disappeared (_ēgī_), some became weak (_fŭgī_> *_fugīī_> fügí); others passed into the _–sī_ or the _–uī_ class: _prehĕndī_> *_prē(n)sī_> pris; _bĭbit_> *_bĭbuit_> bẹc, _vĕnit_> *_vēnuit_> vẹnc. In Provençal only three _–ī_ verbs remained: _fēcī_> fis, _fuī_> füi, _vīdī_> vi.

(3) Of the *-sī* class (including *-ssī* and *-xī*) over twenty verbs were preserved in Vulgar Latin (*dīxī, excŭssī, mīsī, traxī*, etc.), and about the same number passed into this class from others (*absco(n)sī, *fraxī *sŭrsī*, etc.): cf. (1) and (2) above. In Provençal nearly half the verbs of the second and third conjugations have *-sī* preterits: *rema(n)sī* > remas, **re-spō(n)sī* > respọs[1].

(4) The *-uī* class held its own very well in Vulgar Latin (*placuī*, etc.) and received some additions (*natus sum* > **nacuī, sustŭlī* > **tŏluī, vēnī* > **vēnuī, vīcī* > **vīncuī, vīxī* > **vīscuī*, etc.)[2]. To this class belonged, in Vulgar Latin (and, according to Meyer-Lübke[3], in classic Latin also), all perfects in *-vī*, this ending being pronounced -wŭi, later -wwị or -βwị: *cognōvī* > **conōvuī* > conọc, *crēvit* > **crēvuit* > crẹc, *mō-vī* > **mŏvuī* > mọc. Cf. § 148. In Provençal not far from half the verbs of the second and third conjugations have *-uī* preterits. For a combination af a -c < *-uī* stem with a weak ending, see § 175, (3). For the extension of -c < *-uī* to other conjugations, see § 176.

179. In the 1st pers. pl. the accent was shifted to the ending, to make this form correspond to the 2d pers. sg. and pl.: *fēcĭmus* > **fēcímu'* > fezẹm (cf. *fecĭstī* > fezist, *fecĭstis* > fezẹtz), **prē(n)sĭmus* > **presímu'* > prezẹm, *debŭĭmus* > *de-βwímu'* > deguẹm. Exceptions are *fŭĭmus* > fọm, *vīdĭmus* >

[1] All verbs in *-ndĕre* took the perfect in *-sī*: *ascos, aucis, pris, respos*, etc. *Lĕgĕre* took * *lĕxī* > *leis* through the analogy of the p. p. *lĕctum*. So *fingĕre* took **fīxī* > *feis* through *fĭctum*; *frangĕre, pingĕre, tangĕre* did likewise (*frais, peis, tais*); and in Provençal *cénher* < *cĭngĕre, esténher* < *exstĭnguĕre, plánher* <*plan-gĕre* followed the example of these (*ceis, esteis, plais*): hence all verbs in *-nher* have the preterit in *-s*.

[2] See *Zs.*, XXVIII, 97.

[3] *Gram.*, II, p. 357.

vim; in these verbs the 2d pers. forms also are monosyllabic (füst, fọtz; vist, vitz).

180. We find in some verbs an irregular 3d pers. pl. without –r–, made by adding –on or –en to the 3d pers. sg., the final consonant of which is voiced in all verbs in which it is voiced in the other persons of the plural: (aucire) aucis, aucíson; (plánher) plais, pláisson; (prenre) prẹs, prẹson; (remanre) remas, remáson; (venir) vẹnc, vẹnguen; (volẹr) vọlc, vọlgon.

1. *Prenre* has *preiron* (beside *preson preseron*), probably through the analogy of *feiron* < *fēcĕrunt*. *Mairon*, from *maner*, is perhaps to be explained in the same way.

181. (1) Through the change of –ẹ– to –i– by the influence of a final –ī, as described in § 173, (1), a distinction was established between the first and the third person singular of some preterits: *crēvī* > cric, *crēvit* > crẹc; *fēcī* > fis, *fēcit* > fẹs; **prē(n)sī* > pris, **prē(n)sit* > prẹs; *tĕnuī* **tēnuī*[1] > tinc, *tĕnuit* **tēnuit* > tẹnc; *vēnī* **vēnuī*[1] > vinc, *vēnit* **vēnuit* > vẹnc. Mẹtre, also, has mis, mẹs, which may come from **mĭssī* **mĭssit* (cf. *mĭssum*) = *mīsī*, *mīsit*; or perhaps mis comes from *mīsī* and mẹs is analogical. Through the analogy of such forms, quẹrre has quis, quẹs. In the preterit of podẹr, both *pŏtuī* and *pŏtuit* would regularly have given pọc puọc puẹc (§ 37), but pọc was kept for the 3d person, and puọc puẹc was used for the 1st. The preterit of volẹr differentiates the two persons similarly — vuẹlc, vọlc; here the diphthong (perhaps under the influence of puẹc) is borrowed from the present, where we have **vŏleo* > vuẹlh, **vŏlet* > vọl (§ 37). Avẹr, likewise, borrows a distinction from the present: aic, ac reproduce the vowels of ai, a; aic + aguí > aiguí.

[1] *Tĕnuī* and *vēnī* influenced each other.

(2) For -í as a characteristic of the first person, see § 177, (1).

(3) For -c as a distinctive mark of the third person, see § 176.

182. The three -ī **perfects** developed in Provençal as follows: —

(1) *Facĕre* > faire (**fare* > far) has:

fēcī	> fis, fezí	*fēcĭmus *fēcĭmu'*	> fezẹm
fēcĭstī	> fezíst fezís	*fēcĭstis*	> fezẹtz fezẹs
fēcit	> fẹtz fẹs	*fēcĕrunt*	> fẹiron fẹiro

1. We do not find, in the 1st pers. sg., as we should expect (§ 65, C′), *fitz* beside *fis*; doubtless the form came early under the influence of *mis*, *pris*, *quis*, etc. For *fezí*, see § 177, (1). There is also a form *fi*, due, perhaps, to the analogy of *vi* < *vīdī*; corresponding to *fi* are 3d pers. sg. *fe*, and pl. *fem*, *fes*, *feron*. A rare *figuí* is evidently made on the model of *aiguí*, etc. In the 3d pers. sg. we find also *fei*, which seems to be patterned after *feiron* or after the present *fai*.

(2) *Esse* (> **ĕssĕre* > ẹsser ẹstre) had originally a long *u* in the perfect. In literary Latin the *u* was shortened, but the popular speech seems to have kept *ū* beside *ŭ*. The Provençal 1st and 2d pers. sg. apparently come from *fūī*, **fūstī* = *fuĭstī* (although Pr. füi might be taken from *fŭī*), while the other forms presuppose *ŭ*:

fūī	> füi	*fŭĭmus *fŭmu'*	> fọm
*fŭĭstī *fūstī*	> füst füs	*fŭĭstis *fŭstis*	> fọtz fọs
fŭit	> fọ, fọn, fọnc	*fŭĕrunt *fŭrunt*	> fọron fọro, fọren

1. A rare *fo* in the 1st pers. sg. seems to be simply borrowed from the 3d. In the 3d pers. sg., *fon* beside *fo* is due to the analogy of *-on -o* in the 3d pers. pl., and, in general, of such double forms as *bon bo*, *mon mo*, *son so*, *ton to*: cf. § 63, (5). *Fonc* shows the influence of *tenc*, *venc*.

(3) *Vidēre* > vezẹr has:

vīdī	>*viði *við vi, vic	*vīdĭmus *vīdĭmu'*	> *viðmu *viim vim
vīdĭstī	> vist vis	*vīdĭstis*	> vitz vis
vīdit	> *við vi, vit, vic	*vīdĕrunt*	> *viðrun viron viro

1. The 1st pers. sg. *vic* is patterned upon *aic* < *habuī*, *cric* < *crēvi*, etc. The 2d pers. forms are irregular, as we should expect *vezist, *vezetz: evidently the 2d pers. followed the analogy of the 1st and 3d. In the 3d pers. sg., *vit* and *vic* follow the model of *partit*, *partic*, etc.: see § 173, (3), and § 176.

183. In the –sī **perfect** the 3d pers. pl. presented difficulties. If the –e– of the penult fell, an s or z and an r were brought together. Most dialects apparently preserved the –e–, and shifted the accent to it (aucizẹron, condüissẹron, dissẹrọn, prezẹron, remazẹron, traissẹron), or else borrowed outright the weak ending (respondẹron): cf. § 49, (2), and § 177, (3). Dialects which lost the –e– too early to follow this method, generally suppressed the sibilant (aucíron, diron, mẹron from mẹtre, remáron), or omitted the –r– and formed the 3d pers. pl. directly from the 3d pers. sg. (aucízon, pláisson, prẹzon, remázon: § 180), or else imitated a preterit of another class (mairon from manẹr, prẹiron from prenre, doubtless patterned after fẹiron < *fēcĕrunt*); some borderland dialects kept the sibilant and the r, and developed a dental between them (düystrent < *dūxĕrunt*, mẹsdren < *mīsĕrunt* + *mĭssĕrunt: § 70, Sr, Zr).

As examples of the *–sī* perfect we may take the preterit of dire < *dīcĕre* and penre prenre < *pr(eh)ĕndĕre*: —

(1) *dīxī*	> dis, dissí	*dīxĭmus* *dīxĭmu'	> dissẹm
dīxĭstī	> dissíst	*dīxĭstis*	> dissẹtz dissẹs
dīxit	> dis	*dīxĕrunt*	> dissẹron, diron diro
(2) *prē(n)sī	> pris, prẹs, presí	*prē(n)sĭmus *prēsĭmu'	> presẹm
*prē(n)sĭstī	> presíst	*prē(n)sĭstis	> presẹtz presẹs
*prē(n)sit	> prẹs	*prē(n)sĕrunt	> presẹron, prẹson, [prẹiron

(3) Escriure < *scrībĕre* has, beside escris < *scrīpsī*, a preterit escrius (cf. p. p. escriut escrit escrich), in which the u is probably due to the influence of the infinitive.

(4) For dissí, presí, quesí, respozí, see § 177, (1). For pris prẹs, etc., see § 173, (1).

184. In the **-uī perfect** the development depends somewhat upon the consonant preceding the *u*. The treatment of the various cons. + w groups, which was discussed in § 72, may be illustrated by *ha*bu*it* > ac[1], *crēvit* **crē*vu*it* > crẹc[2]; *nŏ*cu*it* > nọc[3]; *sēdit* **sĕ*du*it* > sẹc, *pŏ*tu*it* > pọc; *va*lu*it* > valc[4], *tĕnuit* **tĕ*nu*it* > tẹnc[5], *mĕ*ru*it* > mẹrc; *sa*pu*it* > saup[6]: the noteworthy features are the change of *u* to -c (through w, gw, g), the absorption of the preceding consonant unless it be a liquid, a nasal, or a *p*, the preservation of the liquid or nasal, and the metathesis of the *p*.

Avẹr < *habēre*, podẹr < **pŏtēre pŏsse*, volẹr < **vŏlēre vĕlle*, sabẹr < **sapēre sapĕre* will serve as examples (for the accentuation of the 3d pers. pl., see § 16, 2): —

(1)	*habuī*	> ac, aguí, aic, aiguí	*habuĭmus* **aβwĭmu'*	> aguẹm
	habuĭstī	> aguíst	*habuĭstis*	> aguẹtz aguẹs
	habuit	> ac	*habuĕrunt*	> ágron ágro, aguẹron

1. For *aguí* (*beguí*, *conoguí*), see § 177, (1). For *aic*, *aiguí*, (*cric*), see § 181, (1). For *aguẹron* (*visquẹron*), see § 177, (3).

(2)	*pŏtuī*	> pọc puọc puẹc	*potuĭmus* **potwĭmu'*	> poguẹm
	potuĭstī	> poguíst	*potuĭstis*	> poguẹtz poguẹs
	pŏtuit	> pọc, pọt	*potuĕrunt*	> pọgron pọgro

1. For *puoc*, see § 181, (1). *Pot* is apparently due to the combined influence of weak preterits and the parts of *poder* in which the dental is preserved.

---

[1] So *bĭbuit* > *bec*, *debuit* > *dec*.

[2] So *cognōvit* > *conoc*, *mōvit* > *moc*.

[3] So * *cŏcuit* > *coc*, *jacuit* > *iac*, * *nascuit* > *nasc*, * *pa(s)cuit* > *pac*, *placuit* > *plac*, *tacuit* > *tac*, * *tescuit* > *tesc*, * *vĭncuit* > *venc*, * *vīscuit* > *visc*.

[4] So *caluit* > *calc*, * *tŏluit* > *tolc*, *vŏluit* > *volc*.

[5] So * *vēnuit* > *venc*.

[6] So *erĭpuit* > *ereup*, *recĭpuit* > *receup*.

(3) *vŏluī*	> vǫlc, vuęlc, volguí	*voluĭmus* **volwĭmu'*	> volguẹm
voluĭstī	> volguíst	*voluĭstis*	> volguẹtz volguẹs
vŏluit	> vǫlc	*voluĕrunt*	> vǫlgron vǫlgro

1. For *vuelc* (*tinc*, *vinc*), see § 181, (1); for *volguí* (*venguí*), § 177, (1).

(4) *sapuī*	> saup, saubí	*sapuĭmus* **sapwĭmu'*	> saubẹm
sapuĭstī	> saubíst	*sapuĭstis*	> saubẹtz saubẹs
sapuit	> saup	*sapuĕrunt*	> sáubron sáubro, sáupron

1. For *saubí*, see § 177, (1). For *sáupron* (*sáupra*, *saupés*, *saupút*), see § 65, P, 3; cf. § 148, (2).

OLD CONDITIONAL.

185. The old conditional came from the Latin pluperfect indicative, which had been supplanted in its pluperfect sense by a compound form, and was gradually restricted in its use to the functions of a preterit, a perfect conditional, and a simple conditional: see § 141, (2). In Provençal it had only the conditional meaning; and as the new conditional rendered it superfluous, it fell into disuse (with the exception of ágra and fọra) in the 13th and 14th centuries: see § 142, (2).

186. In the fourth conjugation the old conditional comes from the contracted form of the pluperfect (*audīram* < *audīvĕram*). Weak verbs of the third conjugation constructed a similar form (**vendẹram*). First conjugation verbs started with the contracted pluperfect (*amāram* < *amāvĕram*), but in Provençal substituted ẹ for á, as in the preterit: § 175, (4). The Provençal types of the old conditional of weak verbs are, therefore, represented by: amẹra, vendẹra, auzíra. The inflection is as follows: —

amẹra	amerám	auzíra	auzirám
amẹras	amerátz	auzíras	auzirátz
amẹra	amẹran	auzíra	auzíran

187. Strong verbs of the *-ī* and the *-uī* classes regularly took their old conditional directly from the Latin pluperfect: *fēcĕram* > fẹira, *fŭĕram* > fọra, *vīdĕram* > vira; *habŭĕram* **áβwĕram* (§ 16, 2) > ágra, *pŏtŭĕram* > pọgra, *vŏlŭĕram* > vọlgra, *sapŭĕram* > sáubra sáupra (§ 65, P, 3). Of course the Latin pluperfect, and therefore the Provençal conditional, followed the shift of the perfect if it changed from one class to another: *vēnī* > **vēnuī*, hence **vēnŭĕram* > vẹngra. The inflection is as follows: —

fọra	forám	ágra	agrám
fọras	forátz forás	ágras	agrátz agrás
fọra	fọran	ágra	ágran

1. *Faire* has *féra* (cf. *feron*) beside *féira*.

2. For *sáupra*, cf. §148, (2), and § 184, (4), 1, and § 192.

3. *Devér* has beside *dégra* a form *déura*, evidently influenced by the new conditional, *deuría*.

4. *Páisser*, *plazér* have beside *págra*, *plágra* the forms *paisséra*, *plazéra*.

188. Strong verbs of the *-sī* class regularly form their old conditional on the same plan as the 3d pers. pl. of the preterit (§ 183): (*dīxĕram*) díra, cf. díron; (**prēsĕram*) prẹira, cf. prẹiron; (*arsĕram*) arsẹra, cf. arsẹron.

189. It will be noted that in all verbs, weak and strong, the old conditional may be constructed from the 3d pers. pl. of the preterit by changing -on to -a.

IMPERFECT SUBJUNCTIVE.

190. The Provençal imperfect subjunctive came from the Latin pluperfect subjunctive, which in Vulgar Latin assumed the functions of the imperfect and generally displaced it, its own place having been taken by a compound form: see § 141, (2).

191. For weak verbs the basis was the contracted form of the first and fourth conjugations (*amāssem* < *amāvĭssem*, *audīssem* < *audīvĭssem*); weak verbs of third conjugation had a similar analogical form (**vēndẹssem*). First conjugation verbs substituted ẹ for á, as in the perfect and the old conditional: § 175, (4); § 186. The Provençal types are: amẹs, vendẹs, auzís. The inflection is:

amęs	amessẹm	auzís	auzissẹm
amęsses	amessẹtz -ẹs	auzísses	auzissẹtz -ẹs
amęs	amęssen -on -o	auzís	auzíssen -on -o

192. Strong verbs regularly made their imperfect directly from the Vulgar Latin form of the pluperfect: *fecĭssem* > fezẹs, *fŭĭssem* **fŭssem* > fọs, *vidĭssem* > vezẹs, *venĭssem* **venuĭssem* > venguẹs; *dixĭssem* > dissẹs, **pre(n)sĭssem* > prezẹs; *habuĭssem* > aguẹs, *potuĭssem* > poguẹs, *voluĭssem* > volguẹs, *sapuĭssem* > saubẹs saupẹs (§ 65, P, 3). The inflection is: —

fọs	fossẹm	aguẹs	aguessẹm, acsẹm
fọsses	fossẹtz -ẹs	aguẹsses	aguessẹtz -ẹs, acsẹtz -ẹs
fọs	fọssen -on -o	aguẹs	aguẹssen -on -o

1. The syncopated forms in the 1st and 2d pers. pl. are common to the *-uī* class: *decsém*, *iacsém*, *pocsém*, *saupsém*.

2. In the 3d pers. pl. *-an* sometimes takes the place of *-en* or *-on*: *mezéssan*, *saubéssan*. This ending is doubtless borrowed from the present subjunctive and the old conditional.

3. *Vezér* has *vis* beside *vezés*. From *faire* we find in the 3d pers. pl. *fésson*.

4. *Metre* has *mezés*, due, no doubt, to the analogy of *mes* and of *prezés*.

193. Some dialects have an ending -a, -as, -a, -ám, -átz, an, borrowed from the present subjunctive and the old conditional, but added to the stem of the imperfect subjunctive: chantẹssa, vendẹssa, floríssa; fọssa.

INDEX

N. B. — The references are to paragraphs.

BOOKS FROM TIGER XENOPHON & TIGER OF THE STRIPE

Henry Sweet, *An Anglo-Saxon Primer,* 132pp., paperback, ISBN 978-1-904799-25-2

Henry Sweet, *An Anglo-Saxon Reader,* 420pp., paperback, ISBN 978-1-904799-28-3

Henry Sweet, *The Student's Dictionary of Anglo-Saxon,* 224 pp., paperback, ISBN 978-1-904799-09-2

Joseph Wright, *A Grammar of the Gothic Language,* 380pp., paperback, ISBN 978-1-904799-22-1

Joseph Wright, *A Middle High German Primer,* 228 pp., paperback, ISBN 978-1-904799-26-9

Eduard Prokosch, *A Comparative Germanic Grammar,* 356 pp., paperback, ISBN 978-1-904799-42-2

Benjamin Hall Kennedy, Revised by Gerrish Gray, *Kennedy's New Latin Primer* (UK edn), 264 pp., paperback, ISBN 978-1-904799-18-4

Benjamin Hall Kennedy, Revised by Gerrish Gray, *Kennedy's New Latin Primer* (US edn), 264 pp., paperback ISBN 978-1-904799-19-1

BOOKS FROM TIGER XENOPHON & TIGER OF THE STRIPE

Charles H. Grandgent, *From Latin to Italian: An Historical Outline of the Phonology and Morphology of the Italian Language,* 200 pp., paperback, ISBN 978-1-904799-23-8

Charles H. Grandgent, *An Introduction to Vulgar Latin,* paperback, 240pp., ISBN 978-1-904799-43-6

Charles H. Grandgent, *An Outline of the Phonology and Morphology of Old Provençal,* 176 pp, paperback, ISBN 978-1-904799-27-6

Joseph Anglade, *Grammaire Elémentaire de l'Ancien Français,* 240 pp., paperback, ISBN 978-1-904799-20-7

William Goodwin, *A Greek Grammar,* 492 pp., hardback, ISBN 978-1-904799-21-4
paperback, ISBN 978-1-904799-24-5

Edward Maunde Thompson, *An Introduction to Greek and Latin Palæography,* 616 pp., hardback, ISBN 978-1-904799-30-6

Edward Maunde Thompson, *The History of English Handwriting,* 80 pp., paperback, ISBN 978-1-904799-10-8

www.ingramcontent.com/pod-product-compliance
Lightning Source LLC
Chambersburg PA
CBHW021104090426
42738CB00006B/504
* 9 7 8 1 9 0 4 7 9 9 2 7 6 *